WORLD SERIES COMMEMORATIVE BOOK

THE REST IS HISTORY

BOSTON RED SOX
2018 World Series Champions

This book is available in quantity at special discounts for your group or organization. For further information, contact:

Triumph Books LLC
814 North Franklin Street
Chicago, Illinois 60610
Phone: (312) 337-0747
www.triumphbooks.com

Printed in U.S.A.
ISBN: 978-1-62937-600-4

Content packaged by Mojo Media, Inc.
Joe Funk: Editor
Jason Hinman: Creative Director

Front and back cover photos by USA TODAY Sports Images

Interior photos by AP Images

CONTENTS

2018 World Series

World Series
Game 1 • October 23, 2018 • Boston, Massachusetts
Red Sox 8, Dodgers 4

The Jump Off

Red Sox Overpower Kershaw and the Dodgers in 8-4 Win

A pitching duel turned into another affair altogether in Game 1 of the 2018 World Series, won by the Red Sox 8-4 at historic Fenway Park.

Clayton Kershaw started for the Dodgers, Chris Sale started for the Red Sox – a marquee pitching matchup if ever one existed, right?

Neither offense bought the hype.

Riding a four-game winning streak, the hot Red Sox struck first against the Dodgers' three-time Cy Young Award winner.

Mookie Betts singled to lead off the first then stole second and scored when Andrew Benintendi singled to right. Yasiel Puig's throw from right field missed the cutoff man, which allowed Benintendi to go to second on the play. One out later, J.D. Martinez singled to left to score Benintendi and put the Red Sox up 2-0.

"It started with Mookie putting a good at-bat together, and then just getting ahead early," Benintendi said. "We've been trying to do that all postseason, and for the most part it seems like we've been able to do that so far. Maybe it puts pressure on them right away, but hopefully we can keep doing it."

Facing Kershaw presented several problems to the Red Sox's order.

"Yeah, I mean, obviously we're facing a guy who's one of the best of all time," Benintendi said. "And a lot of guys didn't have a lot of experience off of him; the first time a lot of us have faced him. Didn't really know what to expect."

While the Red Sox didn't know what to expect, Benintendi felt as though his team had a "good game plan."

"We stuck to it," Benintendi said. "It started with Mookie. And just trying to tack on runs one at a time. And we tried not to give away at-bats. And it seemed like for most of the year up until now we've had good at-bats the entire game, and don't give any away. Just to get him in the zone and try not to chase. I don't want to say too much. We'll probably face him again. But we swung at strikes for the most part, and caught a few bad breaks, honestly."

Sale had been hospitalized during the American League Championship Series with an unspecified stomach ailment (True story or not, he told reporters he had an infection due to a belly-button ring). That malady caused the Red Sox ace to miss his scheduled Game 5 start in the ALCS. So, there were concerns about how he might perform in the opening game of the World Series. But the blade-thin lefty started strong, striking out the first two batters he faced.

Matt Kemp got the Dodgers on the scoreboard when he homered with one out in the second. Manny Machado singled home another run in the third to tie the score at 2.

Typifying the Red Sox's season, they answered in the bottom half of the inning when Martinez doubled home Steve Pearce to take a 3-2 lead.

The back and forth would continue in the fifth, with Kershaw and Sale each confronting their own demons.

Mookie Betts scores on an RBI single by Andrew Benintendi during the first inning of Game 1. Betts scored two runs from the leadoff spot in the game.

Sale's came in the form of an elevated pitch count.

Following a strong fourth inning that saw Sale retire the Dodgers in order, two by swinging strikeouts, he walked the leadoff batter in the fifth.

After Brian Dozier took his free pass, Cora went to the mound and signaled for the bullpen. Sale had thrown 91 pitches to that point.

"That was good stuff today," said Cora of Sale. "He did a good job taking pitches and fouling off pitches. But stuff-wise, probably the best in the postseason. And he feels really good, no problems with the belly button. So that's a plus. He'll be okay for the next one."

Matt Barnes took over for Sale in the fifth and the Dodgers pushed across the tying run when Machado grounded out to drive home Dozier.

Once again, the Red Sox answered in the bottom half of the inning. After Mookie Betts drew a leadoff walk, Benintendi singled to left to drive home Betts and chase Kershaw, who struggled with his command.

Above: Andrew Benintendi hits an RBI double off of Clayton Kershaw in the first inning of the Game 1 win. Opposite: The breakdown of Chris Sale's throwing motion during the fourth inning of Game 1. Sale pitched only four innings but did have seven strikeouts in the no decision.

"I don't think he had the fastball command that he typically does, missing up in the zone," Dodgers manager Dave Roberts said. "I don't think his slider had the depth that we're used to seeing. And those guys, to their credit, they put some good at-bats on him. And we didn't play the defense that we typically do. I thought we left some outs out there. And it didn't make Clayton's job any easier."

Ryan Madson took over for Kershaw and surrendered an RBI single to Rafael Devers that pushed the Red Sox's lead to 5-3. The home team would not trail again.

"When you can score right after they score, it kind of takes the breath out of them, or at least that's how we feel I guess if that were to happen to us," Benintendi said. "It's huge. It gets the momentum back on your side."

Pinch-hitter Eduardo Nunez's three-run homer off Alex Wood in the seventh broke open the game, giving the Red Sox an 8-4 lead, which would prove to be the final margin.

"You know, in the beginning I thought it was going to be a single, because the ball [was going] so high and I know it wasn't a slow ball," Nunez said. "And when I see the ball is going, I was excited, because I didn't expect the ball going away.

"...I think that was the best feeling for a player, see all the fans. They paid tickets to watch us to play and be crazy. In that situation I think that's a great feeling for us."

Cora complimented his hitters, noting they had "some good at-bats."

"A lot of good at-bats together," Cora said. "From the first at-bat we put pressure on them. And that's what we do. We stayed off the edges of the strike zone, we attacked pitches in the middle of the zone, and we did an outstanding job offensively." ∎

Eduardo Nunez celebrates as he rounds the bases after hitting a three-run home run during the seventh inning of the 8-4 win.

World Series
Game 2 • October 24, 2018 • Boston, Massachusetts
Red Sox 4, Dodgers 2

Applying Pressure

Price Steps Up Again and Red Sox Take Commanding 2-0 Series Lead

David Price, postseason weapon.

What once sounded like an oxymoron, suddenly sounds like a fact. The veteran Boston left-hander minted that identity in the Red Sox's 4-2 win over the Dodgers in Game 2 of the World Series.

Flash back to the beginning of the Red Sox 2018 playoff journey. Price had started Game 2 of the American League Division Series against the Yankees, and he had lasted just 1 2/3 innings, getting booed heavily by the Fenway faithful.

But the journey had continued to unfold.

Price entered his Game 5 start in the AL Championship Series against the Astros having never won a postseason game in 11 previous starts, and he came through with six scoreless innings of work to pick up his first postseason win in the Red Sox's series-clinching win over the Astros.

Could Price carry over that success to consecutive playoff starts?

He answered that question with two scoreless innings, striking out three of the first seven batters he faced.

The Red Sox grabbed a 1-0 lead in the bottom of the second when Xander Bogaerts kickstarted the Red Sox's seemingly always active offense with a one-out double to center field. Ian Kinsler drove him home with a two-out single to left.

Price added another scoreless frame before the Dodgers got busy in the fourth.

David Freese and Manny Machado cobbled together singles to start the inning, then Price made matters worse by walking Chris Taylor to load the bases. Red Sox manager Alex Cora kept the faith, leaving Price in the game.

Matt Kemp's sacrifice fly tied the score. Price struck out Enrique Hernandez for the second out, then Yasiel Puig singled to center field to give the Dodgers a 2-1 lead, their first lead of the World Series.

Price struck out Austin Barnes to finish the inning.

Escaping that jam "was very important," Price said. "I just told myself to continue to make pitches. I made a lot of good pitches that inning. They hit some. Took some. That was a tough inning, it could have spun out of control pretty fast. And it's been one of my Achilles heels especially in the playoffs and even in the regular season, is that big inning. Being able to stop it at two right there after the Puig hit to center, that was big for us."

Price then retired the Dodgers in order in the fifth.

In the bottom half of the fifth, the Red Sox put together a two-out rally.

Christian Vazquez and Mookie Betts each singled against Dodgers starter Hyun-Jin Ryu in advance of Andrew Benintendi drawing a walk to load the bases. Dodgers manager Dave Roberts opted to bring in Ryan

David Price was terrific in the Game 2 win, going six innings with five strikeouts, while only allowing two earned runs.

Madson to pitch to Steve Pearce. That strategy failed when Madson walked the Red Sox first baseman to force home the tying run.

"That was a great example of just how you grind out an inning, grind out at-bats," J.D. Martinez said. "Everybody, you know, something we preach about. And we were talking about it after the game – after that inning, actually. Underneath, that was such a perfect example of just grinding at-bats out, finding ways to get guys on and keeping the line moving."

Martinez then kept the line moving when he dropped in a single that landed in front of Puig in right. Betts and Benintendi scored on the play and the Red Sox had a 4-2 lead.

"I faced [Madson in Game 1] and it was a very similar situation," Martinez said. "He was a little wild, and I went up there kind of passive. I said, this is the time, I said, trust your eyes. Go up there and trust your eyes and if it's a ball, it's a ball, but don't go up there being passive.

"It wasn't a bad pitch. It was a good pitch. I was just fortunate enough to stay inside of it and dump it in, really."

Puig had been stationed deep in right field for Martinez's at-bat. Roberts defended his positioning.

"I think with the Martinez ball, even if he was in, it's going to drop in," Roberts said. "It's two out, they're running on contact. And you've got to still respect J.D.'s power. But I thought it was an executed pitch that he just got enough of it to muscle it out to the outfield. I don't think the outfield depth really played a factor in that."

Price complimented the effort of the Red Sox offense.

"I think we've been a very good offense all year long with two outs," Price said. "And that's tough to do, whenever that pitcher is one pitch away from being out

of an inning, and be able to have nobody on base with two outs and to start a rally like that, that can deflate teams, so that's huge."

Price took the mound in the sixth. Once again, he retired the Dodgers in order before calling it a night.

Joe Kelly pitched a scoreless seventh. Nathan Eovaldi came through with a scoreless eighth. And Craig Kimbrel recorded the final three outs in the ninth to preserve the 4-2 Red Sox win.

Red Sox pitching retired 16 consecutive Dodgers batters to end the game.

Price's final line read two runs on three hits and three walks while striking out five, and his second postseason win.

Price savored the win, but he thought team first.

Getting the win was "huge," Price allowed. "This is the biggest stage in baseball. There's no other stage that's going to be bigger than pitching in a World Series game, unless it's Game 7 of the World Series. To be able to do that, it feels good, for sure. I'm pumped for myself, pumped for all my teammates and coaches for us to be two wins away, and I'm 2-0 right now in the World Series, that's a good feeling."

Cora allowed that his team had played "two good games."

"Today a tough one," Cora said. "They pitched well. We put some good at-bats. We pitched extremely well. David was amazing. And then the bullpen did what they've been doing during October and now we're up 2-0." ■

Andrew Benintendi leaps and makes an amazing catch in the fifth inning, assuredly robbing Dodgers' Brian Dozier of an extra-base hit.

	W	L	GB
OSTON	108	54	—
EW YORK	100	62	8
MPA BAY	9	72	18
ORONTO	7	89	35
LTIMORE	47	115	61

World Series
Game 3 • October 26, 2018 • Los Angeles, California
Dodgers 3, Red Sox 2 (18 innings)

Hollywood Marathon

Dodgers Take Longest-Ever World Series Game on Muncy Walk-Off

The Red Sox went to Hollywood looking for a sweep. The Dodgers changed the script in Game 3, but they needed 18 innings and the longest game in World Series history to do so to claim a 3-2 win to cut the Red Sox lead to 2-1.

With the score tied 2-2, Max Muncy led off the bottom of the 18th inning, facing Nathan Eovaldi, who was beginning his seventh inning of relief.

The Red Sox righty fell behind 3-0 before a called strike fastball and a foul tip made the count full. Muncy hung tough, fouling off the sixth pitch, a 96.2 mph four-seamer, to set the stage for his epic blast.

Eovaldi delivered a 90.1 mph cutter and Muncy connected, depositing the ball into the left-center field stands 382 feet from home plate for the game winner.

"The feeling was just pure joy and incredible excitement," Muncy said. "That's about all I can think of because it's hard to describe how good a feeling it is."

Muncy's blast ended the 7 hour, 20 minute game. Putting that time into perspective, the New York Yankees took less time (7 hours 5 minutes) to sweep the Cincinnati Reds in 1939 in four games.

"The effort was amazing," Red Sox manager Alex Cora said. "It was a great baseball game. Seven hours, whatever it is. People back home are probably waking up to the end. But it's probably one of the best, if not the best, game I've ever been a part of. The effort from both sides.

"What Nate did tonight, that was amazing. That was amazing. We kept talking to him, 'I'm good. I'm good. I'm good.'"

Eovaldi had allowed no earned runs in his previous six innings of work, and he had a chance to win the game in the 13th.

The score had been tied at 1 when the fateful 13th inning began.

Brock Holt scored in the top half of the inning on a throwing error by Dodgers pitcher Scott Alexander, leaving the Red Sox three outs away from taking a commanding 3-0 series lead.

Instead, the Red Sox returned the favor with their own fielding gaffe with two outs in the bottom of the 13th.

Eovaldi walked Muncy to start the inning and one out later third baseman Eduardo Nunez caught Cody Bellinger's pop out in foul territory. Nunez fell into the stands while making the catch. According to the rulebook, the ball was dead after the play and the baserunner was entitled to a free base. Thus, Bellinger advanced to second base with two outs.

Yasiel Puig followed with a grounder through the middle that second baseman Ian Kinsler fielded, then threw wild to first, allowing Bellinger to score and tie the game at 2.

"It seemed like he was a little off balance when he caught it," Cora said. "He's one of the best defensive second basemen in the big leagues. He's been making

The Dodgers mob Max Muncy after his walk off home run mercifully ends the 18 inning Game 3 marathon.

that play for a while and just threw it away."

Eovaldi then retired Austin Barnes to send the game to the 14th inning.

Eovaldi allowed just two baserunners in the four innings that followed, leading to the 18th. By that point, he'd thrown 90 pitches.

Thinking to himself that he'd allow Eovaldi to pitch one more inning, Cora spoke to the veteran when he returned to the dugout after retiring the Dodgers in the 17th.

"When he came in, I asked him, 'How do you feel?'" Cora said. "He's like, 'Let me finish it.' And I'm like, 'Okay.' I don't know if I told him, 'You've got one more.' Drew [Pomeranz] was up already. Actually Drew was going to hit at the top of the next inning, whatever it was. So his stuff was still good. The last out, Turner, that was good. And then Muncy put a good swing on it, and hit it out of the ballpark."

Rick Porcello started for the Red Sox and pitched two scoreless innings before Joc Pederson homered to right field with two outs in the third to put the Dodgers up 1-0.

One run normally would not look like a large obstacle to overcome for this Red Sox collection, but Walker Buehler was dealing.

The Dodgers' starter held the potent Red Sox offense scoreless on two hits while striking out seven in seven innings.

"I think that certain people can handle a moment like this and understand what was at stake tonight," Dodgers manager Dave Roberts said. "And we needed his best effort. And we needed him to go deeper than their starter, log some innings. And some guys run from it. Some guys can't answer the bell. But this guy, he's got an overt confidence, a quiet confidence, a little

combo. But he's got tremendous stuff. And he lives for moments like this."

Buehler had used 108 pitches to that point, prompting Roberts to go to the bullpen.

Kenley Jansen entered the game to start the eighth inning and retired Holt and Rafael Devers to bring Jackie Bradley to the plate.

Bradley's heroics had earned him MVP honors during the American League Championship Series. Once again, he came through, homering to right field to tie the score at 1.

Boston had a chance to go ahead in the 10th when Nunez flew out to center field with one out and Kinsler on third. Bellinger caught the ball and threw a strike to the catcher, Barnes, who tagged out Kinsler trying to score.

"We're down 2-1, but I think that the crowd tonight was outstanding," said Roberts, referencing the Dodger Stadium crowd of 53,114. "Was loud from before the first pitch, and we anticipated that. So to get in front of 50,000 Dodger fans to drive us and to stay for, what was is 17 innings, 18, 19, 7 hours and 20 minutes, and there were still probably fans here. So the way that our guys, our pen, got the outs that they needed, and they did a heck of a job." ∎

Eduardo Nunez is upended by catcher Austin Barnes while Barnes tried to field a wild pitch during the 13th inning of Boston's 3-2 loss.

World Series
Game 4 • October 27, 2018 • Los Angeles, California
Red Sox 9, Dodgers 6

Never Give Up

Red Sox Storm Back to Take Commanding 3-1 Series Lead

Refusing to quit has been a consistent quality of the 2018 Red Sox. Never was that more apparent than in their 9-6 come-from-behind win in Game 4 of the 2018 World Series.

A night after losing Game 3 in walk-off fashion to the Dodgers in an 18-inning, 7 hours and 20 minutes contest, the Red Sox fell behind 4-0 when Yasiel Puig put the Dodgers up 4-0 in the sixth inning.

On the surface, the Dodgers appeared on the verge of storming back to tie the series at two games. Perhaps after taking two straight they'd even win Game 5 and carry a 3-2 series lead back to Boston.

The only people who didn't believe such a situation would come to fruition were the players in the visiting dugout at Dodger Stadium.

Both teams' pitching was running on fumes entering the game, thanks to the previous night's marathon. Red Sox manager Alex Cora certainly left himself vulnerable for the critics after burning Nathan Eovaldi in Game 3. Eovaldi pitched six-plus innings in that appearance, and obviously could not start Game 4. That prompted Cora to start Eduardo Rodriguez.

The left-hander had pitched the night before, but only for 1/3 of an inning. So Cora handed him the ball and Rodriguez pitched well, posting five scoreless innings before taking the mound in the sixth inning of the scoreless game. That's when things began to unravel for Rodriguez and the Red Sox.

David Freese led off the inning, and Rodriguez hit him with a pitch before striking out Max Muncy for the first out. Justin Turner then doubled to left and Rodriguez intentionally walked Manny Machado to load the bases. After Cody Bellinger grounded into a force out to drive home a run, Puig stepped to the plate with runners at the corners and Rodriguez fell behind the Dodgers slugger 3-1.

Had Cora left Rodriguez in the game too long?

Puig provided the answer to that question when he connected on a 92-mph two-seamer and deposited the ball 439 feet into the left-field center-field stands.

Puig flipped his bat, held up his arms, then performed the baseball equivalent of a touchdown dance as he circled the bases, flexing his muscles as he returned to the Dodgers dugout.

Rodriguez had a different response, as he slammed his glove on the mound.

"I pushed [Rodriguez] too hard," Cora said. "I had Joe [Kelly] ready, I had Barnesie [Andrew Barnes] ready, Turner, we felt that we could get a ground ball. ... Turner tucks one down the line. We walk Machado. We make a great pitch to Bellinger. We don't get the double play, they scored one. We felt the matchup [with Puig] was

Brock Holt reacts after hitting a double in the ninth inning of the Game 4 win. Holt had a hit and drew two walks in the game.

good for us, that matchup is good for us when Eddie is fresh, and he's able to get that fastball up."

Puig's blow put the Dodgers up 4-0, and the momentum of the series continued to shift in their direction.

Rich Hill started for the Dodgers and pitched six scoreless innings before the Red Sox began to answer in the seventh. If anybody knew anything about this Red Sox team, they knew they would not go quietly into the night.

Xander Bogaerts drew a leadoff walk to start the seventh and one out later, Dodgers manager Dave Roberts changed pitchers, bringing in Scott Alexander to face Brock Holt.

Holt walked, and Roberts brought in Ryan Madson to pitch to pinch-hitter Jackie Bradley, who popped out for the second out. Cora then sent pinch-hitter Mitch Moreland to the plate and he delivered a three-run homer that cut the lead to 4-3.

"Anytime you come up with a situation like that, you want to make something happen," Moreland said. "But we had two guys go up there and build an inning before me, and just we kept grinding and kept grinding, and finally gave ourselves an opportunity by putting some guys on base and able to capitalize and get a good pitch in and put a swing on it."

Steve Pearce homered in the top of the eighth to tie the score at 4, setting the stage for additional heroics from Pearce in the ninth.

Holt doubled with one out in the ninth and scored on Rafael Devers' single to center to put the Red Sox ahead at 5-4.

Mookie Betts was intentionally walked with two outs before Andrew Benintendi loaded the bases with an infield single to bring Pearce to the plate.

Once again, the veteran slugger came through, driving a double to center field that cleared the bases.

Bogaerts added a single to drive home Pearce to complete the five-run ninth.

Pearce is "a good at-bat," Cora said. "He doesn't expand. He stays in the zone and able to go the other way. Like today he was out in front of the first one, then gets a fastball and shoots it the other way. He's a complete player. He's a complete hitter. Very mature. The moment, it's not too big for him."

Craig Kimbrel entered to pitch the bottom of the ninth and allowed a two-run homer to Enrique Hernandez before settling down to record the final three outs, and the Red Sox had a come-from-behind 9-6 win.

"With our mindset, we can change a game quick," Moreland said. "We play 27 outs or however many was [in Game 3]. We're going to grind it until the last out, the last pitch, and we've proven that all year. We've had a lot of come-from-behind wins. We can throw a big inning together pretty quick.

"It's a special group. Our offense has done some stuff that I don't know, but I'm pretty sure there's not too many teams that have done what they've been able to do over the course of the year. It's been special to be a part of and to see what we can accomplish. And I think tonight was just another example of that. Obviously, we put ourselves right where we need to be. And we've got one more to go. So that's our mindset right now."

The Red Sox did not panic. ∎

Mitch Moreland watches his three-run home run off of Ryan Madson in the seventh inning. The long fly got the Red Sox on the board and opened up the floodgates on offense on the way to a 9-6 win.

World Series
Game 5 • October 28, 2018 • Los Angeles, California
Red Sox 5, Dodgers 1

Damage Done!

Red Sox Finish Off Dodgers, Cap Greatest Season with World Series Crown

The Red Sox clinched their fourth World Series title in 15 seasons with a 5-1 win over the Dodgers in Game 5. Prior to the first of those four titles, the Red Sox went 86 years without winning a World Series.

Chris Sale struck out Manny Machado for the final out in the ninth inning, prompting a celebration to break out on the Dodger Stadium infield. The team that had won 108 games during the regular season had closed the deal.

The Dodgers, who lost to the Houston Astros in the 2017 World Series, could only watch from their spot in the home dugout.

The Red Sox did a lot of winning during 2018.

Following their 108-54 season, they won 11 more games during the postseason, putting them at 119 wins. Only the 1998 New York Yankees, who had 125 wins en route to winning the World Series, and the 2001 Mariners, who won 120 games but did not reach the World Series, won more times.

The Red Sox were remarkably consistent throughout the regular season, and they continued to be that way in the postseason. They only lost three times in the playoffs: once to the Yankees in the American League Division Series, once to the Astros in the American League Championship Series, and once to the Dodgers in the World Series.

Red Sox hitters backed a quality start by David Price with four home runs.

World Series MVP Steve Pearce hit two home runs while Mookie Betts and J.D. Martinez chipped in one each. Meanwhile, Price picked up his second win of the World Series after holding the Dodgers to one run on three hits and two walks while striking out five in seven innings.

"[The win is] very special," said Price in an on-field interview following the win. "Seeing all these grown men over there acting like little kids, that's what it's all about."

The 33-year-old lefty allowed that the 2018 season, and what happened in the World Series was "why I came to Boston."

Price, who threw an inning in relief in Game 3 after throwing 88 pitches in his Game 2 start, was pitching on short rest as Sale was moved to Game 6. By picking up his second win of the World Series, and third of the postseason, Price officially retired the narrative that he could not win games in October.

Andrew Benintendi got the Red Sox started with one-out single in the first. Pearce then homered to give the Red Sox a 2-0 lead.

"You've got to strike early [against Kershaw]," Pearce said. "You saw how he settled in in the middle innings. And, yeah, just to be able to get my pitch and not miss it, and give us an early lead, that was big for our club."

David Freese answered for the Dodgers by hitting Price's first pitch of the game over the right-field fence to cut the lead to 2-1.

Price walked the next batter, Justin Turner, before

David Price was brilliant once again, this time going seven innings while only allowing one earned run, and delivering another championship to the city of Boston.

getting Enrique Hernandez to ground into a 5-4-3 double-play. Manny Machado then struck out to end the inning.

Price needed 38 pitches to get through the first two innings before settling into a rhythm that saw him use just nine pitches in the third and nine in the fourth.

The Dodgers threatened in the third when Freese tripled with one out after Martinez misplayed the ball. That easily could have turned into Price's undoing, but he remained unfazed, answering the challenge by retiring Turner on a ground out and Hernandez on a fly out to end the inning without allowing any runs to score.

After the Freese triple, Price retired the next 14 batters he faced before walking Chris Taylor to start the eighth.

"You know, I've said it every single time I've been asked about Price, is we love him," Pearce said. "When he's on the mound, we have the utmost confidence in the guy. He's a bulldog, he's competitive, and he wants to win. When he's on the mound, we feel that, and we're confident playing behind him."

Added Dodgers manager Dave Roberts: "You've got to give credit to David Price over there. He pitched a heck of a ballgame. Couldn't put hits together, couldn't

Opposite: Mookie Betts watches his home run off of Clayton Kershaw during the sixth inning of the clinching win. It was his first home run in 87 career postseason at-bats. Above: The Red Sox celebrate after Chris Sale closes the door on the Dodgers and clinches the ninth World Series title in franchise history.

get baserunners, and really stress them at all. It was pretty straightforward. I can't say enough about what Clayton – what our guys did. And unfortunately, we came up short again this year."

Like Price, Kershaw also appeared to be settling into a groove as he faced the minimum in the four innings following the two-run first. But after retiring Price on a groundout to start the sixth, Betts stepped to the plate riding a 0-for-13 stretch.

Kershaw went 2-2 to Betts before throwing an 89-mph slider that Betts hit over the wall in left.

For Betts, it was his first postseason home run in 87 at-bats.

Martinez, whose bat had also been somewhat chilly during the World Series, then led off the seventh with a solo home run to center off Kershaw that pushed the Red Sox's lead to 4-1.

Pearce's second home run of the game, and third of the World Series, came in the eighth off Dodgers righty Pedro Baez and gave the Red Sox a 5-1 lead.

Joe Kelly then took over.

The hard-throwing Kelly had seemingly found another gear during the World Series, and he continued to operate at the same high level, striking out in order Matt Kemp, Joc Pederson, and Cody Bellinger to finish off the eighth.

Sale, who would have started Game 6 if necessary, entered the game in the ninth and did like Kelly, striking out the side. The veteran left-hander struck out Turner, Hernandez, and Machado all swinging.

"Yeah, you have to give credit to the Red Sox," Kershaw said. "They're a great team. They won, I think, 108 games in the regular season. They beat two teams that also won a hundred games in the postseason. And then beat us four games to one. So, they're a great team, obviously. They have a lot of depth up and down the lineup. You saw guys, their starters out of the bullpen starting, short rest, whatever they did, their bullpen guys throwing the ball great. They're a great team." ∎

World Series MVP Steve Pearce hits his second home run of the night, this one coming in the eighth inning and providing some extra insurance in Boston's 5-1 win.

MVP

Steve Pearce Powers Sox Down the Stretch, Seizes MVP Honors

Steve Pearce was named the World Series Most Valuable Player after providing critical offense to the Red Sox's effort, particularly in the final two games of the series.

"You know, baseball is a funny game," Pearce said. "You never know where the game will take you. And I've gone through a lot in my life or in my career to be here, and I couldn't be more thankful."

In the final two games of the series, Pearce went 4-for-8 with three homers, seven RBI, and four runs scored.

Pearce homered twice in the clinching Game 5, giving him a .333 average for the Series (4-for-12) with a 1.167 slugging percentage.

In Game 4, Pearce hit a game-tying home run in the eighth inning, followed by a three-run double in the ninth to pace the Red Sox to a 9-6 win.

All told, Pearce hit three home runs and a double, driving in eight and scoring five.

"Best feeling in my life," Pearce said. "This is what you grow up wishing that you could be a part of something like this. With that special group of guys out there, to celebrate with them, that was awesome."

Pearce came to the Red Sox in a June 28 trade with the Blue Jays. He becomes the second World Series MVP who joined a team as an acquisition at mid-season. Donn Clendenon was named the 1969 World Series MVP when the Mets defeated the Orioles in the Fall Classic. The Mets had acquired Clendenon in June of the 1969 season.

Pearce, 35, is a well-traveled veteran, and had played for every team in the American League East before finding his way to the Red Sox roster in 2018.

"One of the favorite things I've seen when I've been here was the team chemistry on and off the field," Pearce said. "And when I came in it was having fun and laughing, everyone was together and talking baseball. And then you notice on the field when you're playing against them for so long, they're always having fun. And it's very contagious, and it's just a great atmosphere over there."

After the Red Sox lost 3-2 in an 18-inning affair in Game 3, their offense remained in idle for most of Game 4. Pearce's bat helped change that narrative.

"Yeah, we had about 20 innings of sluggish baseball," Pearce said. "Our offense wasn't responding. We were just not playing well, but the pitchers did great. Everybody in the bullpen and we fought and then it was the big blow by Mitch kind of started everything going. And I think that's what we needed. We just needed some kind of spark to help us out. Once we got it, I think everybody kind of felt the momentum started to shift in our favor, and we started to play our baseball."

Pearce joined Babe Ruth and Ted Kluszewski as the only players 35 or older with multiple-homer games in a World Series. When asked if it meant something to be mentioned with Babe Ruth in the annals of the World Series, Pearce replied: "Sure, that's great company. Those guys were the best. And if my name gets to sit right next to theirs, I know I've accomplished something." ■

Steve Pearce was a mid-season acquisition from the Blue Jays that paid off in historic fashion in the World Series, as he homered three times and drove in eight runs.

ROAD TO
THE TITLE

The Blueprint
How to Build a Championship Team in 2018

Having the ability to identify talent, and being able to procure that talent, has had everything to do with the Red Sox's success. Players win championships.

Here's a look at how the 2018 Red Sox were built.

Acquired through free agency were the following:

Ryan Brasier, J.D. Martinez, Mitch Moreland, and David Price. Xander Bogaerts and Rafael Devers signed as international free agents.

Martinez had posted a monster 2017 season with the Detroit Tigers and Arizona Diamondbacks when he hit 45 home runs in 119 games. Such numbers normally would have commanded more on the free agent market – and he still got a lot of money – but the Red Sox got a bargain when they signed Martinez five-year, $110 million deal in late February. He went on to hit .330 with 43 home runs and 130 RBI.

Price signed a seven-year, $217 million contract prior to the 2016 season and has since gone 39-19 with a 3.74 ERA in 81 appearances.

Point being, the Red Sox aren't afraid to spend money on free agents. And when they have done so, they have done well at signing players who performed.

Players acquired through trades include: Nathan Eovaldi, Heath Hembree, Brock Holt, Joe Kelly, Craig Kimbrel, Ian Kinsler, Sandy Leon, Eduardo Nunez, Steve Pearce, Rick Porcello, Eduardo Rodriguez, and Chris Sale.

Sale came to the Red Sox in a 2016 trade that sent Luis Alexander Basabe (minors), Victor Diaz (minors), Michael Kopech, and Yoan Moncada to the Chicago White Sox.

The Sale trade personified the importance of developing a strong minor league system. You must have players who project to become quality major leaguers in order to have the assets to acquire a talent of Sale's ilk.

Pearce, Kinsler, and Eovaldi all came to the team prior to major league baseball's 2018 trade deadline. Each has proven to be a valuable pickup, particularly Eovaldi.

The Red Sox acquired Eovaldi from the Tampa Bay Rays for pitching prospect Jalen Beeks. He went on to go 3-3 with a 3.33 ERA in 12 appearances (11 starts), logging 54 innings.

Acquired through the draft were the following:

Matt Barnes, Andrew Benintendi, Mookie Betts, Jackie Bradley, Blake Swihart, Christian Vazquez, and Brandon Workman.

Speaking of being able to identify talent, the Red Sox drafted the following in the 2011 draft: Barnes, Swihart, Bradley, and Betts.

A pretty good haul, highlighted by Betts, who the Red Sox grabbed in the fifth round with the 172nd pick of the draft.

That group from the 2011 draft played together throughout the minor leagues, which proved valuable to their development as well as the Red Sox's.

"They all came up together," Red Sox manager Alex Cora said. "They won a lot in the minor leagues and they knew each other. It really helps in the clubhouse. I think like nowadays it's not like when I came up that the veterans, they were tough on first-year players. Now it's not as tough. Actually, I tried to make sure the first-year players are included, you know. Like I don't mind a first-year player to come to my office and tell me how he feels about the lineup or something that we should do, because at the end of the day he's part of what we're trying to accomplish.

"But for them to come up together I bet there were some great conversations in A-ball, eight-hour trips, about playing together in the World Series and winning the championship for the city and the Boston Red Sox, and now they have the chance."

Of note, the Red Sox had the seventh pick of the 2015 draft and selected Benintendi, illustrating the importance of making the right selection when you have a high pick. ∎

J.D. Martinez, right, smiles alongside David Dombrowski, president of baseball operations, during a news conference announcing his five-year, $110 million deal.

MANAGER

MANAGER

ALEX CORA

Cora Makes History with Good Vibes and Consistency

On October 17, 2017, Alex Cora became the 47th manager in Red Sox history, signing a three-year deal to manage the team through the 2020 season with a club option for 2021.

At the time of the announcement, Cora served as the bench coach for the Houston Astros, who were about to begin a seven-game World Series appearance against the Los Angeles Dodgers. Ironically, those Astros won the World Series, as did the Red Sox in Cora's first season managing the team.

Cora played parts of 14 seasons in the Major Leagues with the Dodgers, Red Sox, Mets, Rangers, Nationals, and Indians. A utility player, Cora hit .243 with 35 home runs and 286 RBI in 1,273 major league games. His final season in the major leagues came in 2011 for the Nationals.

During his run with the Red Sox from 2005-2008, he became a part of the 2007 World Series championship club.

Red Sox general manager Dave Dombrowski interviewed three candidates for the job of succeeding John Farrell as the team's manager. Also interviewed were Brad Ausmus and Ron Gardenhire.

In taking the job, Cora became the 22nd former Red Sox player become manager. Butch Hobson had been the last former player to manage the club, which he did from 1992 through 1994.

Among Cora's skill set were his intelligence and his ability to work with young players. His experience included being general manager for the Criollos de Caguas in the Puerto Rican Winter League. In addition, he served as the team's manager for two seasons. Cora also was the general manager for the Puerto Rico team that finished second in the 2017 World Baseball Classic.

Cora received media polish from his four years as a baseball analyst for ESPN and ESPN Deportes.

By becoming a major league manager, Cora became the first in major league history to hail from Puerto Rico.

"I'm proud to be here," said Cora prior to the start of the 2018 World Series. "I'm proud representing not only all the Puerto Ricans that live in the island, but Puerto Ricans all around the world. We know what happened last year [with the hurricane devastation incurred]. It was a tough one. And Maria kicked our ass, you know. As a country, we've done an outstanding job fighting. We're standing up on our own two feet. I know there's a lot of people back home they're proud of me, of what I've done throughout the year. But

First-year Red Sox manager Alex Cora watches his players practice during Spring Training in Fort Myers, Florida.

I'm proud of them. We actually – it's almost back to normal. Almost back to normal."

Cora's tenure got off to an auspicious beginning when the Red Sox began the 2018 season with a 17-2 record. The team would post a 108-54 regular season record to win the American League East en route to winning the World Series.

Cora becomes the fifth first-year manager in major league history to win the World Series in his first season. Bob Brenly last accomplished the feat as the manager of the Arizona Diamondbacks in 2001.

Cora allowed that making decisions was one of the tougher aspects of his job.

"Sending guys down, taking them out of the lineup," Cora said. "The Hanley [Ramirez] situation, that was a tough one. And it's not easy. It's not easy. It's always cool to give guys good news. But it's always tough to give guys bad news. And throughout the season you have to do that and that's the tough part.

"But we have a job to do as an organization and you have to make moves that you feel that are going to benefit what we're trying to accomplish. But that's the tough part. That's a very tough part of the job."

But there are the happy moments, too. Like when the Red Sox clinched the ALCS on October 18, Cora's 43rd birthday. His players sang happy birthday to him during the clubhouse celebration.

Throughout the postseason, Cora shined, whether he was making the right move with the bullpen or showing faith in a struggling player. Clearly, Cora is a favorite in the clubhouse.

David Price spoke about how Cora has harped on humility and the togetherness of the team.

"That was one of the things that Cora talked to us about, just going out there and playing the game the right way," Price said. "I feel like Boston has played the game the right way ever since I've been here. Just a lot of times they're better than anybody else, they get under your skin and they have a bigger payroll. I feel like teams with lesser payroll could kind of resent the Red Sox in that way.

"…And we've played very good baseball all year long. And AC has led us extremely well. So he deserves a lot of this credit."

Chris Sale spoke highly of Cora's consistency.

"He's the same guy in the first inning as he is in the ninth inning of a 10-1 ballgame or 3-3 ballgame," Sale said. "I think that's the overall thing as players that we take from him, or me personally, I don't want to speak for everyone else, it's just his composure, being the ninth inning, bases loaded, one out of a one-run ballgame, and he's sitting there eating seeds, doing the same thing as a 10-1 ballgame in the fourth inning. And I think that goes very well with us as players, when if he's not panicking, why should we? If he's calm, cool and collected, so should we. And I think that's kind of been the overall consensus throughout the years.

"He's been a good leader and we've been able to feed off of his vibes, and he's had nothing but good vibes the whole year." ■

Alex Cora's steady and calm demeanor was the perfect fit for this Red Sox squad.

50

RIGHT FIELDER

Mookie Betts

Betts Does It All for Red Sox, Has That MVP Feel

In the top of the third inning on September 30, 2018, a Fenway Park crowd of 36,201 felt appreciative on the final day of the Red Sox season. The Red Sox led the Yankees 7-0 after two turns at bat, putting the hometown team well on its way toward nailing down its 108th win of the season. Manager Joey Cora seized the moment to honor Mookie Betts, who had contributed as much as anybody to the Red Sox's swollen win total.

Betts stood in right field awaiting the start of the inning when the Red Sox manager directed Tzu-Wei Lin to right field to take over for Betts. When Betts started toward the Red Sox dugout, the Fenway faithful began their chant, "M-V-P! M-V-P!"

Betts certainly ranked as the favorite to win the American League MVP award. Whether or not he would win the award remained to be seen, but he'd done everything he could to compile an impressive enough résumé to earn said standing.

Betts raked from the beginning of the year.

During the Red Sox's 17-2 run to start the season, Betts served as the catalyst from the leadoff spot, hitting a Major League-leading .382 batting average. Included in that body of work was a three-homer game against the

Angels on April 17. By doing so at age 25, Betts became just the third player in major league history to have three career three-homer games before turning 26, joining Hall of Famer Ralph Kiner and Boog Powell.

Further accomplishments during the Red Sox's torrid opening stretch were Betts' 1.234 OPS, two games in which he led off with a homer, and his 23 runs. Dating back to 1908, that run total ranked as the second-most runs scored by a Red Sox player in the first 19 games. Only the "Splendid Splinter" – Ted Williams, scored more when he crossed the plate 24 times in the Red Sox's first 19 games of 1942.

Betts continued to hit throughout the Red Sox's record-setting season. During the season, he and teammate J.D. Martinez held their own friendly competition for the AL batting title. Ultimately, Betts claimed the batting crown with a .346 average (which also led the major leagues), while Martinez finished second at .330. Not since 1942, when Ted Williams led the AL with a .356 average and Johnny Pesky finished second at .331 had the Red Sox had the top two hitters in the league.

Betts and Martinez seemed to feed off each other's success all season long.

Mookie Betts is a true five-tool player, excelling in every aspect of the game, including as a leader.

Betts had 30 stolen bases on the season, tying him with Dee Gordon for fifth most in the American League.

"Yeah, I think it was one of those things where our personalities are so similar that we're just always talking hitting and always wanting to, like, get better and work," Martinez said. "And so it's one of those things that it's almost like – I don't know how to explain it – it's like we're always in the cage together hitting, and we're always pushing each other in that sense, like, oh, what do you have on this, what do you have on that type deal and kind of game planning and getting ready for a pitcher.

"I don't know, it's cool because I've been on many different teams, and you don't really find like personalities that are similar when it comes to passion for hitting as when I found him."

Betts allowed that he learned a lot from Martinez, who was in his first season with the Red Sox.

"I could sit here all day and talk about what I've learned, but the most important thing is to trust your work," Betts said. "I mean, I go in and put in so much work. Like I said, we put in so much work and you have to go and trust it. I mean, I think that's the most important thing that I've learned for sure."

Betts' .346 average was the highest by a Red Sox hitter since 2002 when Manny Ramirez hit .349.

Bill Mueller had been the last Red Sox player to win a batting title when he hit .326 average in 2003. No Red Sox player had led the major leagues since Wade Boggs had done so with a .366 average in 1988.

Betts' led the major leagues in runs and slugging percentage. In addition, he had 30 home runs and 30 steals.

While Betts' offense overshadowed everything, he played Gold Glove defense in right field.

Yes, Mookie Betts is a complete player, who had a complete season. Sounds like an MVP. ∎

Betts and teammate J.D. Martinez battled all season for the AL batting title, with Betts prevailing with a .346 average.

Blazing Fast

The Historic Start to the Season Set the Tone for the Greatness Ahead

Opening Day for the 2018 season found the Red Sox in St. Petersburg playing the Tampa Bay Rays.

The March 29 game looked well in hand when the Red Sox took a 4-0 lead into the bottom of the eighth at Tropicana Field.

Chris Sale started for the Red Sox and the standout lefty had held the Rays scoreless on one hit and three walks through six innings, striking out nine in the process. Well on his way to his first win of the season.

Then the bottom fell out.

After Matt Barnes pitched a scoreless seventh, Joe Kelly took over, allowing four runs while getting just one out in the eighth. Carson Smith then took over and allowed the big blow to Denard Span, who tripled with the bases loaded.

By the time the third out of the eighth was recorded, the Rays had scored six times in the inning to earn a 6-4 win.

Tampa Bay's miraculous win brought panic to Red Sox Nation. Were they heading into the season with a paper bullpen? Could this team fulfill the promise forecast for it? And what about new manager Alex Cora? Could he push the right buttons to lead the club to a world championship?

With David Price leading the way, Boston regrouped to defeat the Rays 1-0 the next night, igniting the start of an historic run.

The Red Sox won their final two games against the Rays then went south to Miami, where they defeated the Marlins in consecutive games before heading to Boston for the home opener against the Rays. They swept the Rays in three games at Fenway Park before hosting the Yankees, winning three of four. Baltimore then came to town and the Red Sox swept the Orioles in three games before leaving for a trip to the West Coast. First, they swept the Angels in three before they traveled to Oakland to play the A's, holding a record of 16-2.

On April 20 at Oakland, Jackie Bradley Jr. hit a three-run homer and Mitch Moreland hit a grand slam to lead to a comfortable 7-3 Red Sox win over the A's. That moved the Red Sox to 17-2 on the season and on to hallowed ground.

The Red Sox finally had their streak snapped the next night in Oakland in a 3-0 loss. The loss allowed time for reflection on just what the Red Sox had accomplished.

During the 17-2 stretch, the Red Sox outscored opponents by a margin of 70 runs – including five grand slams, while hitting .293 as a team. The run wasn't fueled by offense alone. Red Sox starters wemt 12-1 with a 2.17 ERA and the bullpen allowed just one run in 25 1/3 innings through the team's 17th win. Five of the 17 wins came by one run.

Eduardo Nunez loses his helmet as he races around third base for a two-run, inside-the-park home run off Tampa Bay Rays starting pitcher Chris Archer in the season opener. The Red Sox lost the game but would go on to win the next nine in a row.

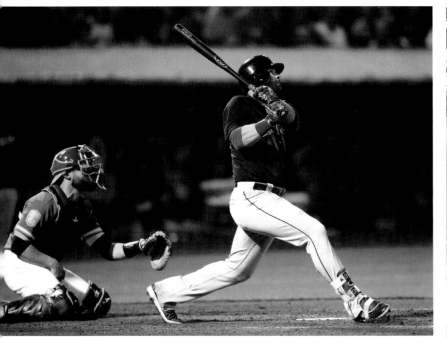

Only seven teams in major league history (since baseball's modern era, 1900) had managed to start the season by winning 17 of their first 19 games. And no team had turned the trick since the 1987 Milwaukee Brewers.

The other teams to experience 17-2 starts include the 1984 Detroit Tigers, the 1981 A's, the 1955 Brooklyn Dodgers, the 1918 New York Giants, and the 1911 Tigers. The 1918 Giants actually went 18-1 to start the season.

Not since 1988 had the Red Sox enjoyed a 17-1 run (remember they lost Opening Day) over an 18-game stretch. That '88 squad cashed in its hot streak to storm back into the American League East race. They would win the division that season. The 1946 Red Sox also enjoyed a stretch that saw the team win 17 of 18 games.

Going 17-2 to start the season set the tone for a season in which the Red Sox finished with 108 wins – another franchise best. ■

Above: Mitch Moreland watches his grand slam against the Athletics on April 20 during a win over Oakland that moved Boston's record to 17-2. Opposite: Hanley Ramirez celebrates after hitting a walk-off single to beat Tampa Bay in 12 innings on April 5.

41

STARTING PITCHER

Chris Sale

Red Sox Ace Finds a Way to Get It Done Amidst Drama

Chris Sale reigned as one of the top pitchers in baseball – and the left-hander became available after finishing the 2016 season, his seventh season with the Chicago White Sox. Red Sox president Dave Dombrowski understood the kind of talent Sale represented, and acted accordingly, orchestrating a blockbuster trade on December 6, 2016 to send a package of quality prospects to Chicago for the White Sox ace.

Sale had been a five-time All-Star with the White Sox and boosted an elite Red Sox staff that already included Cy Young winners David Price and Rick Porcello.

In seven seasons with the White Sox, Sale went 74-50 with a 3.00 ERA and 1,244 strikeouts in 1,110 innings pitched. He'd been dominant throughout, and he continued to dominate once with the Red Sox.

In two seasons with the Red Sox, Sale has gone 29-12 with a 2.56 ERA in 59 starts. But his 2018 season got shortened by two stints on the disabled list in late July and mid-August due to shoulder inflammation.

During a 108-win season where little went wrong for the 2018 Red Sox, the status of Sale's shoulder remained a concern, bringing forth the most drama of

the season to Red Sox Nation. Even when Sale came off the DL on September 11, the drama continued.

Upon his return, he made restricted starts of one inning, three innings, 3 1/3 innings, and 4 2/3 innings. In those starts, Sale's fastball wasn't the same, averaging 92.8 mph rather than the 98 mph he showed in June and July. By his final start of the regular season, that average fell to 90.2.

Sale's slider looked as wicked as ever, but he struggled with command. He attributed all of his problems to mechanical issues. Still, that made the staff ace the Red Sox's biggest question mark heading into the postseason.

Manager Alex Cora didn't seem to have any doubts about what Sale could do, and the Red Sox manager penciled him in to start Game 1 of the American League Division Series against the Yankees. Sale didn't seem to have any concerns, either.

"If I take the mound I expect to win," said Sale when asked about his velocity. "I don't care what I have on a given day, I should be able to find a way with whatever I have. In terms of what that was, it's a game, what are you going to do? Sometimes you go out there and you have your best, sometimes you don't. This is sport. This is

Chris Sale was a true ace for the Red Sox in 2018, with a 2.11 ERA and 237 strikeouts in 158 innings pitched.

baseball. You have to find a way with whatever you have on any given day and roll with it."

Sale went out and pitched 5 1/3 innings, holding the Yankees to two runs on five hits while walking two and striking out eight.

"I felt more like myself because I felt like this was just a normal start," Sale said. "Not normal in terms of not being a postseason start, but just like there's no restrictions. There's no going out to the bullpen after my start to add pitches. I knew I was going to get my 100-plus pitches or somewhere around there. That's a very freeing feeling."

Sale next pitched a one-inning relief stint in the deciding Game 4 and retired the Yankees in order in the eighth inning.

Drama over? Not yet.

After making a four-inning start against the Astros in Game 1 of the American League Championship Series, Sale had to be hospitalized with a stomach illness and did not travel with the team to Houston.

Would he make his scheduled Game 5 start? Nope.

Cora opted to bump his ace to either Game 6 of the ALCS, or Game 1 of the World Series if they eliminated the Astros in Game 5, which they did.

Sale later told reporters that the cause of his stomach problems stemmed from a belly-button ring that he'd constantly taken in and out, which caused an irritation. He also didn't specify whether he was joking when he cited that ailment for the cause of him being hospitalized.

But Sale returned to the mound to start Game 1 of the World Series, and he had a so-so performance, allowing three runs on five hits and two walks while striking out seven in four innings of the Red Sox 8-4 win over the Dodgers.

"That was good stuff today," Cora said. "…stuff-wise, probably the best in the postseason. And he feels really good, no problems with the belly button. So that's a plus." ∎

Sale is one of the most unique personalities in baseball, from cutting the collars off of throwback jerseys in the locker room with the White Sox to missing a scheduled ALCS start because of stomach irritation from "a belly-button ring."

Chris Sale has established himself as one of the best pitchers of his generation and now has a World Series ring to add to his trophy case.

The Fab Five
Red Sox Rewarded for Dominant First Half with Five All-Stars

Based on how the Red Sox played in the first half of the 2018 season, having five Red Sox players named to the 2018 American League All-Star team's roster wasn't much of a surprise. Alex Cora informed the team about the All-Star selections during a team meeting that took place in the visiting clubhouse in Kansas City. What brought a surprise to the gathering was the Red Sox manager's announcement that Mitch Moreland would be among the five Red Sox players headed to Nationals Park in Washington, D.C. for Major League Baseball's big event. The veteran first baseman joined the likes of Chris Sale, Mookie Betts, Craig Kimbrel, and J.D. Martinez.

The surprise in the Red Sox clubhouse shouldn't have been construed as a knock against Moreland's abilities, rather an expression of joy. His teammates were happy for him and they cheered accordingly.

Moreland found his way onto the team via the players and coaches vote.

There had been doubts that Moreland would be back with the Red Sox in 2018, and he wasn't even considered a starting player at the beginning of the season. Things quickly changed after the Red Sox released Hanley Ramirez on May 30.

Moreland had hit .321 in April and .300 in May before moving into a starting role following the Ramirez move.

"That was cool," Cora told MLB.com. "We talked about it before the game. There's a guy that in the offseason, a lot of people didn't think he was going to be here for X or Y reason. We decided to make a commitment with him. He didn't start the season as an everyday player. He earned it. We made a huge move because we wanted him to play every day. Out of all of them – I'm very proud of all of them – but to tell the team that he's an All-Star, that was amazing."

For Sale, he earned his seventh selection to the All-Star Game. Sale went 10-4 with a 2.23 ERA in 20 starts prior to departing for the Nation's Capital.

Betts and Martinez each posted superlative offensive numbers in the first half, which saw the Red Sox head to the break in first place with a 4 1/2 game lead after posting a scorching 68-30 mark.

Betts went into the All-Star break hitting .359 with 23 home runs and 51 RBIs, including a .691 slugging percentage and a 1.139 OPS.

Martinez entered the break with a .328 average, 29 home runs and 80 RBIs, slugging .644 with a 1.037 OPS.

Kimbrel had a 2-1 mark with a 1.77 ERA and 30 saves.

Martinez made his second All-Star team, Betts his third, and Kimbrel his seventh.

Martinez received 3,035,619 votes in the fan voting while Betts received 4,286,994 votes, second only to Jose Altuve for the most votes received by an AL player.

Fellow All-Stars J.D. Martinez, left, and Mookie Betts, both had huge offensive years and found themselves consistently discussed as MVP candidates.

When Sale arrived in Washington, D.C., American League manager A.J. Hinch told him of his decision to make him the AL's starting pitcher. During the media day prior to the big event, Hinch addressed the reporters with Sale alongside him at the podium, affording him the opportunity to explain why he'd selected Sale to start.

"Some tough choices around the league," Hinch said. "There are a number of guys that I considered but, honestly, the proof is in the numbers and the most consistent starter in the American League. You like wins, you like games, you like consecutive six-inning outings, just pure dominance, you like a punch. We've seen a few of those. He's truly a special pitcher in this league and truly someone who deserves this honor.

"He will be starting his third consecutive All-Star Game, which I think is the first time since maybe 1935. A little research for you. But proud to hand you the ball, Chris, and for you to be the American League starting pitcher."

Sale became the third All-Star to start three consecutive All-Star Games, joining a pair of Hall of Famers in Lefty Gomez and Robin Roberts, who had turned the trick.

Sale would do his part for the AL effort, pitching a scoreless inning, allowing a first-inning hit to Javier Baez, and striking out Paul Goldschmidt swinging.

Sale had a couple of familiar faces joining him. Betts went 0-for-3 while playing right field and Martinez started at DH, going 1-for-2. Moreland later took over at first base and went 2-for-3 in his first All-Star Game.

Kimbrel did not see action in the American League's 8-6 win in 10 innings. ■

Five All-Star selections for the Red Sox was a sign of the accolades to come, including the ultimate prize of a World Series crown.

DESIGNATED HITTER

J.D. Martinez

Martinez Rewards Boston's Investment and Then Some

After a long dance between the Red Sox and J.D. Martinez, the veteran slugger signed a five-year deal for $110 million to play for the Red Sox on February 26, 2018.

Martinez had put up video game numbers in 2017. In 119 combined games with the Detroit Tigers and Arizona Diamondbacks, he hit 45 home runs with 104 RBI, slugging at .690 with a 1.066 OPS.

No doubt, Martinez figured he would break the bank once he hit free agency. Now, $110 million is nothing to sneeze at, but that number came in south of what most estimated he'd get, which likely explains his opt-out clauses after the 2019 and 2020 seasons.

The Red Sox had signed their slugger, but the question of whether he'd be a disgruntled slugger had to be floating around in the minds of Red Sox Nation. By the end of the 2018, such a suggestion appeared ridiculous.

In his first season with the Red Sox, Martinez nearly won the Triple Crown, hitting .330 with 43 home runs, and 130 RBI. Martinez finished first in the American League in RBI, second in batting average, and second in home runs.

Flash back to 2013 when Martinez played for the Astros and hit just .250 with seven home runs, and 36 RBI, and his 2018 numbers don't seem real.

"What stands out to me [from his time in Houston]? I think the growing pains, really," Martinez said. "I think I learned how to fail, if that's something. I think I went through all my failure there and I kind of learned and I grew. And I knew kind of what worked, what didn't work."

Martinez credits his poor performance in Houston – and the Astros' decision to release him in March of 2014, for properly motivating him going forward.

"How much does it drive me? I think my failures in Houston is what made me who I am," Martinez said. "I think it's given me that drive, that drive to keep working… I mean, I learned a lot from Houston. And you know what, it made me who I am and there's really no animosity there. In a sense they did me a favor by allowing me to leave and going to play on another team. And if it wasn't for that I probably wouldn't be here right now. Who knows where I would have been?"

Martinez signed with the Tigers that same spring.

"And then I just – after that it was I thank God, gave me another opportunity and put me in a good situation

J.D. Martinez hits an RBI double against the Los Angeles Dodgers during the third inning of Game 1 of the World Series. It was more of the same for Martinez, who had two hits and two RBI in the win.

with Detroit," Martinez said. "And that's kind of where I continued to grow until where I am today, really."

Martinez hit .300 with 99 home runs, and 285 RBI in four seasons with the Tigers before they traded him to the Diamondbacks on July 18, 2017 for Dawel Lugo and minor leaguers Sergio Alcantara and Jose King.

In addition to getting better habits at the plate, Martinez had to find a way to keep on weight throughout the season, and he continues to fight that battle.

"It's definitely something that I work on, I battle a little bit with," Martinez said. "Me and Yoshi [strength & conditioning coordinator Kiyoshi Momose] in there, I kind of let him know day one and he makes me these big old

Opposite: J.D. Martinez was an indispensable part of the lineup, slugging 43 home runs and 130 RBI. Above: Mookie Betts, left, greets J.D. Martinez at the dugout after Martinez's solo home run in a game against the Yankees on August 4, 2018.

shakes right before I go home, weight-gainer shakes so I don't lose weight. It's kind of our little joke that we have on the side. But, yeah, it's one of those things that I battle, and it's something I'll continue to battle through my career."

While Martinez is known as a slugger, and he definitely has the numbers to back that label, he's also a proven hitter, and he came through with one of the Red Sox's biggest hits of the season in Game 2 of the World Series.

In the bottom of the fifth inning with the game tied at 2, Martinez stepped to the plate with the bases loaded. He delivered an opposite-field single that scored Mookie Betts and Andrew Benintendi to give the Red Sox a 4-2 lead, which would equal the final margin.

"You know, it's a big argument in baseball, big topic that everybody wants to talk about," Martinez said. "We always talk about just focusing on obviously we want the ball in the air as hitters, here. We're not up there trying to hit everything in the air and swinging for the fences. We go up there and the pitch dictates what we're going to do.

"We're not up there forcing balls in the air. I feel like it's the common mistake with hitters these days. And I think it's something that we all talk about and we have a really good understanding of it, where we kind of think we're hitters before sluggers in a sense. And that's how I think. I take pride in hitting and being – not just a one-dimensional hitter, a complete hitter. And it's something we all talk about."

J.D. Martinez is a slugger, a hitter, and it turns out, a pretty darn good free-agent signing. ∎

J.D. Martinez was released by the Astros in 2014, which proved to be a turning point in his career and ultimately landed him a World Series ring with the Red Sox.

2

SHORTSTOP

Xander Bogaerts

Bogaerts Bides His Time with Sox, Breaks Out in 2018

Xander Bogaerts is the sleeping giant of the 2018 Red Sox.

When the Red Sox's offense is mentioned, J.D. Martinez and Mookie Betts normally dominate the conversation. But how about the Red Sox's slick-fielding shortstop, who actually swings the bat?

Not only did Bogaerts hit .288 in 136 games in 2018, he chipped in 23 home runs and 103 RBI, producing a pretty sweet turn-around season for the native of Oranjestad, Netherlands Antilles.

After getting hit on the right wrist in a July 6, 2017 game against the Tampa Bay Rays, Bogaerts played through it, even though the disabled list was likely the wiser option. He continued to play even though swinging the bat irritated his injury. He finished the season hitting .272 with 10 home runs and 62 RBI, but clearly, his performance was affected.

Fully healed in 2018, Bogaerts started the season hot, hitting two grand slams in April. He added another to give the Red Sox a walk-off win against the Toronto Blue Jays on July 14.

Bogaerts' slam against the Blue Jays fit the script the 2018 Red Sox followed all season. The Red Sox rarely made mistakes, but when they did, somebody usually found a way to compensate. Bogaerts' big hit helped to erase a base-running blunder by Blake Swihart in the seventh inning.

His third grand slam of the season was Boston's first game-ending grand slam in extra innings since Hall of Famer Jim Rice did so on July 4, 1984.

Bogaerts came to the Red Sox as an international free-agent signing in 2009 at age 16. By the end of the 2013 season, he had arrived with the Red Sox, making his major league debut on August 20, 2013. He played well enough in 18 games – hitting .250 with a home run and five RBI – that he made the Red Sox postseason roster and was able to enjoy being a part of a World Series-winning team. He played in 12 postseason games and hit .296 with two RBI.

"I think it's been awesome," said Bogaerts when asked about his growth and the growth of his Red Sox teammates. "I think a lot of the other guys have matured a lot. I can definitely speak for myself, my first year, I mean I can remember it as if it was yesterday, playing with all those veteran guys.

"But I think this year we [had] the same group. This [season was] the third time [they went] to the

Xander Bogaerts had his best season yet in 2018, hitting .288 with 23 home runs and 103 RBI.

playoffs with the same group. And I think everyone's just used to each other and being able to trust each other a lot more."

Bogaerts proved to be a model of consistency in 2018, averaging an RBI every 4.98 at-bats, and a home run every 22.3 times he stepped to the plate. Like most players in the Red Sox's lineup, Bogaerts has mixed his ability to drive the ball while still making consistent contact. He's also embraced manager Alex Cora's philosophy of being more aggressive.

"Sometimes I want to swing at the first pitch," Bogaerts said. "But it's not always – it's in my DNA. Sometimes I just don't feel that comfortable. But obviously it's something that he's preached a lot to most of the guys on our team. I think in certain situations it's good to use that plan.

"Sometimes I'm not that type of guy. I like to work at an at-bat. I feel more comfortable the more pitches I see, stuff like that. But sometimes it works."

Sometimes that aggressiveness worked for Bogaerts like it did in Game 4 of the American League Championship Series when he had a first-pitch RBI single in the fifth inning against Josh James that tied the game at 4.

"I think this [postseason] I've definitely taken a little bit of a different approach," Bogaerts said. "Also not trying to hit too many homers. As I said, I don't think in the playoffs it's ideal to try to swing for the fence. You're just not going to get results. Even if you get one it's going to be one good result in 10 at-bats. And I don't think it's beneficial to the team.

Red Sox Nation has seen Bogaerts mature from the 21-year-old who arrived in 2013 to the 2018 version. The sleeping giant shortstop is now one of best players in the major leagues.

While Bogaerts is known for his bat, he can also flash the leather, shown here diving for the ball in a September 19, 2018 matchup with the Yankees.

16

LEFT FIELDER

Andrew Benintendi

Benintendi Lives Up to the Hype, Just Getting Started

A snapshot of just who Andrew Benintendi the ballplayer is came in the bottom of the ninth inning of Game 4 of the 2018 American League Championship Series.

The Red Sox led the Astros 8-6, and the best-of-seven series 2-1. Winning the game meant everything to the Red Sox and even more to the Astros, who hoped to tie the series.

Craig Kimbrel began to struggle. After retiring the first batter of the inning, the Red Sox closer walked the next two. One out later, he walked Tony Kemp to load the bases, bringing Alex Bregman to the plate.

The always dangerous Bregman connected and sent a sinking line drive to left field. Benintendi could play the ball safely on one hop, and the Astros would have tied the score. If he didn't play the ball safe and tried to make a diving catch, he ran the risk of missing the ball and having it roll to the wall, allowing all three runners to score and giving the Astros the win.

Benintendi went for it, diving to make the catch. When Red Sox fans breathed again, their left fielder clutched the baseball. Game over and the Red Sox had a 3-1 series lead.

"You know, [the play] was right in front of me,"

Astros manager A.J. Hinch said. "I had a perfect view of it... So when the ball was hit, two parts I was looking at how Benintendi was closing and whether or not it was going to drop in as a – a little more shallow.

"But as he dives, we're all waiting in anticipation. And then his reaction was a pretty aggressive celebration, so I assumed he caught it. We checked the video. And he caught it cleanly. The difference in that game literally was a couple inches. He misses that ball and if it hits leather, he probably keeps the game tied. If it doesn't then the game's over and we're celebrating."

Added Red Sox manager Alex Cora: "Beni took a shot. Had a great jump. And he got it. And now we're up 3-1 against a tough team."

Benintendi plays like his hair is on fire, which is part of what attracted the Red Sox to drafting him in the 2015 draft.

If a silver lining existed from the disastrous 2014 Red Sox season – a season that saw a 78-84 finish – it was the fact the Red Sox earned the seventh pick of the June 2015 draft.

Benintendi was still on the board when the time came for the Red Sox to pull the trigger on their first pick. They selected Benintendi.

Andrew Benintendi broke through on offense in 2018, hitting .290 with 16 home runs and 87 RBI.

Benintendi had been a standout at Madeira (Ohio) High School, earning recognition as the ABCA/Rawlings National High School Player of the Year and Ohio Gatorade Baseball Player of the Year after hitting .564 with 12 home runs, 57 RBI, and 38 stolen bases during his senior season. The Cincinnati Reds noticed Benintendi and drafted him in the 31st round of the 2013 draft. Rather than sign, he opted to attend the University of Arkansas, where he started as a freshman. At the end of the 2015 season, Benintendi's name could be found at the top of the Southeastern Conference leader board with a .380 batting average, 19 home runs, a .489 on-base percentage, and 47 walks.

Benintendi was honored accordingly as the SEC Player of the Year and Baseball America's College Player of the Year. He also won the Dick Howser Trophy and the Golden Spikes Award.

After the Red Sox paid Benintendi a $3.6 million signing bonus, he blew through the organization's farm system. In 151 minor league games, he hit .312 with 20 home runs, 107 RBI, 26 steals, and 103 runs. He made his major league debut on August 2, 2016.

He played in 34 games for the Red Sox in 2016, hitting .295 with two homers and 14 RBI. After that, he became a mainstay for the Red Sox, hitting .271 in 2017 and .290 in 2018.

How dynamic of a player is Benintendi? How about the way he reached base in 10 straight plate appearances in early July, hitting a homer, two doubles, and three singles, and had four walks. Or flash forward to Game 1 of the 2018 World Series when he had four hits, three of them against Dodgers ace Clayton Kershaw.

And Benintendi is just 24, which bodes well for the Red Sox for years to come. ■

Benintendi scored 103 runs on the season, placing him sixth highest in the American League.

The Best Around

Sox Stake Their Claim as the Best Team in Franchise History

Nobody saw this one coming.

Yeah, everybody knew the 2018 Red Sox were going to be good, after all, the 2017 team had won 93 games and the American League East, but 108 wins in 2018? That just didn't seem possible.

On Sunday afternoon, September 30, 2018, the Red Sox hosted the Yankees at Fenway Park in their final game of the regular season. Based on how the season had unfolded, finding the Red Sox in the midst of a three-game losing streak felt as rare as a unicorn sighting. A loss to Baltimore in the middle of the season's final week began the "skid", then the Yankees came to town and won the first two games of the three-game series in advance of Sunday's finale.

Boston had long ago clinched the American League East division – their third consecutive title – and with the best record in baseball, they would have home-field advantage in the playoffs, which were right around the corner. The final game of the regular season really didn't matter, right? Like hell it didn't matter, these Red Sox remained a hungry team. Winning had sustained them all season long, like blood does a vampire. So, they went out and got to work, scoring four in the first and three in the second. In the fourth J.D. Martinez connected off Justus Sheffield with two aboard, depositing his 43rd home run of the season over the wall in right-center

field, thereby putting on ice a 10-2 Red Sox win.

In winning, Boston notched its 108th win of the season – establishing a team record for wins in a single season – and snapped its losing streak, which wasn't a surprise since they had not lost four in a row all season, making them the only team in baseball to avoid doing so. Twice before the Red Sox had gone without losing four-straight in a season. In both of those seasons, 1903 and 2013, they had won the World Series.

After the way this Red Sox team began the season, nothing should have been a surprise.

The team's first win of 2018 came at Tropicana Field, where the Red Sox won three-out-of-four games in their opening series. That paved the way to an epic 17-2 run, giving the Red Sox their best start in franchise history and one of the best starts in major league history.

Playing .882 baseball just isn't a reality for a 162-game major league season, but the Red Sox continued to play exceptional baseball, finishing with an awe-inspiring .667 winning percentage.

Not only did the Red Sox improve by 15 wins over their 2017 total, they became just the 12th major league team since 1900 to win as many as 108 games in a single season, and just the seventh American League team to do so. In franchise history, only three previous Red Sox teams had won as many as 100 games.

Rookie manager Alex Cora recorded the second-

Nathan Eovaldi proved to be a huge mid-season addition for the Red Sox, with a 3.33 ERA in 12 appearances, including 11 starts.

highest win total for a rookie manager. Only Ralph
Houk with the 1961 Yankees had more. Fueled by Roger
Maris and Mickey Mantle, that team won 109 games.

The 1912 Red Sox had held the franchise standard
for wins in a single season. Fenway Park opened its
doors that season, and the Red Sox, managed by Jake
Stahl and led by pitcher Smoky Joe Wood and center
fielder Tris Speaker, went 105-47.

In 1946, a Red Sox collection that included Ted
Williams, Johnny Pesky, Dom DiMaggio, and Bobby
Doerr came close to breaking the 1912 club's mark but
lost its final two games of the season to finish with a 104-
50 record.

Expansion mandated that the 154-game schedule be
lengthened to 162 games, first in the American League
in 1961, then in the National League in 1962. Since a
162-game schedule came into existence, just eight teams
had won as many as 105 wins in a season, and no team
prior to the 2018 Red Sox had done so since the 2004 St.
Louis Cardinals went 105-57.

Boston ran away from the rest of the AL East teams,
including the Yankees, who won 100 games, but finished
eight games behind the Red Sox in the standings.
Baltimore brought up the rear of the division at 47-115,
finishing 61 games out of first.

Quite a season for the 2018 Red Sox. ■

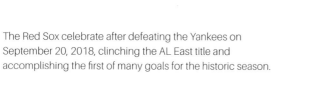
The Red Sox celebrate after defeating the Yankees on
September 20, 2018, clinching the AL East title and
accomplishing the first of many goals for the historic season.

American League Division Series

American League Division Series
Game 1 • October 5, 2018 • Boston, Massachusetts
Red Sox 5, Yankees 4

First Blow

Red Sox Hang On for Hard Fought Win, Take Series Lead

Red Sox-Yankees remains one of the sporting world's more intense rivalries. So a lot of anticipation greeted the American League East rivals entering Game 1 of the 2018 AL Division Series.

The Red Sox posted a 108-54 record during the regular season to win the AL East. Meanwhile, the Yankees went 100-62 to finish second in the AL East and earn a Wild Card spot in the playoffs against the Oakland Athletics. Following a one-game playoff, the Yankees advanced to play the Red Sox.

A raucous Fenway Park crowd of 39,059 watched as the Red Sox got busy early, scoring three runs in the first against Yankees starter J.A. Happ via a J.D. Martinez three-run homer.

"You know, obviously it was important to get that lead right away," Martinez said. "And I think it kind of took a little pressure off everyone. Any time you go into the playoff game everyone's adrenaline is high and tensions are going, stuff like that. I think giving [starter] Chris [Sale] that lead, being able to let him settle in and go out there and pitch, I think definitely just helped relax everybody."

Martinez's blow provided a nice cushion for Sale, who posted zeroes for the first five innings. And Boston's hitters continued to attack.

In the bottom of the fifth, Steve Pearce had an RBI single and Xander Bogaerts's sacrifice fly scored another to push the lead to 5-0.

But Sale found trouble in the sixth when Aaron Judge singled and one out later Giancarlo Stanton followed suit, prompting Red Sox manager Alex Cora to bring in Ryan Brasier, who couldn't put out the fire. By the time Brian Workman – Boston's third pitcher used in the sixth – struck out Gleyber Torres to end the inning, New York had cut the lead to 5-2.

New York further trimmed the lead to 5-3 in the seventh when Luke Voit grounded into a force to drive home a run.

Boston's bullpen looked shaky at best when Craig Kimbrel entered the game to get the final out of the eighth. The Red Sox closer then returned to the mound in the ninth to try and record the final three outs.

Judge greeted Kimbrel with a homer to lead off the inning, moving the Yankees to within one run at 5-4. Then Kimbrel got tough, striking out Brett Gardner, Stanton, and Voit to preserve the Red Sox win.

Sale got the decision to earn his first-ever postseason win, while the Red Sox went up 1-0 in the best-of-five series.

Chris Sale limited the Yankees to two earned runs over 5 1/3 innings, with eight strikeouts.

All told, the Red Sox needed five relievers to get the job done, including scheduled Game 3 starter Rick Porcello.

"I'll take this one," Sale said. "Yeah, I mean, it's postseason baseball. You have to be prepared for anything. We obviously have a lot of faith and trust in our guys. This is baseball, though. Anything can be thrown at you."

Added Martinez: "This is the playoffs. From here on out everything starts at zero. Look at scoreboard, all your numbers are zero, zero, zero. So you know what's at stake. You know what the situation is. You're playing the Yankees." ■

Opposite: Opposite: Jackie Bradley Jr. dives for a single by New York Yankees' Aaron Judge during the seventh inning of the Game 1 win. Above: Second baseman Ian Kinsler forces Brett Gardner out at second during the seventh inning.

American League Division Series
Game 2 • October 6, 2018 • Boston, Massachusetts
Yankees 6, Red Sox 2

Poor Form

David Price Struggles and Bats Go Quiet in Game 2 Loss

Homers led the way as the Yankees evened the American League Division Series with a 6-2 win in Game 2.

After the Red Sox claimed the first win of the series, the rivals returned to Fenway Park for Game 2, with David Price toeing the rubber for the Red Sox.

Though Price had been a successful pitcher during the regular season, he had never experienced success in the postseason. Of all of the southpaw's bad postseason outings, this one took the cake as he lasted just 1 2/3 innings after surrendering three runs – including home runs to Aaron Judge and Gary Sanchez. The home runs were the 10th and 11th Price gave up to the Yankees in 17 1/3 innings against them in 2018. In the process, he managed to raise his postseason ERA to 6.03.

Judge's 445-foot home run gave the Yankees a 1-0 lead in the first. Sanchez's homer came when leading off the second. Two outs later, Price walked Gleyber Torrez and Brett Gardner to set the table for Andrew McCutchen, who singled home the third run and chasing Price. As the veteran hurler made his exit, boos echoed throughout Fenway Park.

"It's tough," Price said. "You know, just after we won Game 1 to go out there and have that opportunity to go up 2-0. And to throw the baseball the way that I did, it was definitely tough. But my spirits aren't down, my confidence isn't down. I'm looking forward to getting back out there and getting another opportunity."

Boston had a chance to get back into the game. Xander Bogaerts hit a solo home run off Yankees starter Masahiro Tanaka in the fourth to cut the lead to two runs. And the Red Sox's troika of relievers, Joe Kelly, Ryan Brasier, and Brandon Workman posted four scoreless innings to move the game into the seventh with the same two-run margin separating the teams. That's when the Yankees put the game away.

Judge greeted Eduardo Rodriguez with a leadoff single in the seventh. Luke Voit drew a walk, then Sanchez unloaded his second home run of the game, giving the Yankees a five-run cushion.

Ian Kinsler answered with an RBI double in the seventh to cut the lead to four runs, but the Yankees' bullpen effort of Dellin Betances, Zach Britton, and Aroldis Chapman shut down the Red Sox's bats.

At the end of the night, the Red Sox had just five hits, and Tanaka picked up the win for his five-inning effort.

"We expanded tonight," said Alex Cora of Tanaka's success. "His split was a lot better. He made some pitches early in the game, and compared to the last one that we had against him, we were very disciplined in New York, and not tonight. We expanded and he did a good job. It seems like when we had him on the ropes when the counts were in our favor, he got back in the count and he threw a split or a slider and we expanded." ∎

Mookie Betts went hitless and the Red Sox only scored 2 runs in their Game 2 loss.

David Price had a short outing in Game 2, only lasting 1 2/3 innings and giving up three earned runs.

American League Division Series
Game 3 • October 8, 2018 • New York, New York
Red Sox 16, Yankees 1

Spin Cycle

Red Sox Take Yanks to the Cleaners, Move One Game Away from ALCS

What little suspense remained in Game 3 of the American League Division Series came in the ninth inning when Brock Holt batted with a chance to hit for the cycle.

If Holt could connect for a home run he would achieve the rare baseball feat.

By the time Holt stepped to the plate, most of Yankee Stadium had cleared out. After all, who wanted to stick around to see the home team get it handed to them, while a reserve infielder tried to hit a home run against Austin Romine, the Yankees' backup catcher?

Holt batted with a runner aboard and two outs, and he managed to connect, sending a drive down the right-field line that cleared the wall to complete the last leg of the cycle. In doing so, he became the first player in major league history to hit for the cycle in a postseason game, and he completed the scoring in the Red Sox's 16-1 win, giving them a 2-1 lead in the series.

"He's been swinging the bat well for a while now," Red Sox manager Alex Cora said. "We felt the matchup was good for him tonight although he was 0-for-whatever coming into the game tonight against [Yankees starter Luis] Severino. He's been able to catch up with fastballs headed the other way, breaking balls, and pull it with power. He's a good player."

Holt led off the fourth with a single off Severino. In that inning, the Red Sox scored seven times and sent 11 hitters to the plate – Holt added a two-run triple off Chad Green in the inning, as the Red Sox took a commanding 10-0 lead.

"It just snowballed on [Severino]," Yankees manager Aaron Boone said. "[Reliever] Lance [Lynn who got just one out] had a little bit of trouble, obviously, coming in there. So it just turned into a really bad inning for us."

Stephen Tarpley was pitching in the eighth when Holt hit an RBI triple, leaving him just a homer away from the cycle.

Holt's line at the end of the night: 4-for-6 with five RBIs and three runs scored.

Boston finished with 18 hits after they had collected just five in Game 2.

Lost in the massacre was the performance of Red Sox starter Nathan Eovaldi, who held the Yankees to one run on five hits while striking out five in seven innings. Not only did Eovaldi pick up the win, he gave the bullpen a much-needed rest a game after David Price had lasted just 1 2/3 innings in his Game 2 start.

Brock Holt follows through on a triple against the Yankees during the fourth inning of Game 3.

"We trust the guy," Cora said. "His stuff is that good. His fastball, 99, 100. The cutter, 94, 95. The split. And one thing with him, it really doesn't matter. Like this stage, you guys saw it. It was unbelievable before the game and the first few innings, and he was just being Nate.

"Pitching in Tampa [where Eovaldi began the season pitching for the Tampa Bay Rays] or pitching in Fenway or pitching in Yankee Stadium, he knows his stuff is good, and it's just about executing, throwing strikes, and letting the defense do the job." ■

Opposite: Boston Red Sox infielders wait for a review of a play during the fourth inning of Game 3 of the ALDS. Below: Clockwise from top left: Brock Holt connects for a base hit in the fourth inning, hits a ground-rule double in the eighth inning, hits a two-run triple in the fourth inning, and follows through on a two-run home run in the ninth inning, becoming the first player to hit for the cycle in a postseason game.

Brock Holt was all over the field and played the game of his life, shown here on the turf after making an off-balance throw to first base in Boston's 16-1 rout of New York.

American League Division Series
Game 4 • October 9, 2018 • New York, New York
Red Sox 4, Yankees 3

Start Spreadin' the News

Sox Dispatch Rival Yankees, Advance to ALCS to face Astros

Game 4 of the American League Division Series came down to one play with two outs in the bottom of the ninth.

What happened next allowed the Red Sox to claim a 4-3 win and advance to the AL Championship Series.

Holding a 4-1 lead at Yankee Stadium entering the bottom of the ninth, Red Sox manager Alex Cora sent in Craig Kimbrel to nail down the final three outs of the game. The Boston closer's outing did not go smoothly, to say the least.

Nothing good happens when the pitcher walks the leadoff batter. That's how Kimbrel's outing began as he walked Aaron Judge. Didi Gregorius followed with a single to right.

The powerful Giancarlo Stanton then stepped to the plate with a chance to tie the game with one swing. Kimbrel recovered to strike out the Yankee slugger swinging before he walked Luke Voit to load the bases.

Making matters worse, Kimbrel then hit Neil Walker with a pitch to force home a run. And still, the bases were loaded with just one out and the Yankees now trailed by just two runs.

Gary Sanchez's sacrifice fly to left moved the Yankees to within one run. Rookie Gleyber Torres had

a chance to be the hero but could only manage a roller down the third-base line.

Third baseman Eduardo Nunez scooped up the ball and snapped off a quick throw to first. Steve Pearce stretched to make the catch. First base umpire Fieldin Culbreath signaled out.

Not satisfied with the call that would end their season, the Yankees challenged. After a 63-second review, the out call was upheld, and the Yankees were eliminated.

Rick Porcello started for the Red Sox and picked up his first postseason win after limiting the Yankees to one run during his five innings of work.

Supporting Porcello's effort, Red Sox hitters pushed across three runs against Yankees starter CC Sabathia in the third. J.D. Martinez started the scoring with a sacrifice fly. Ian Kinsler had an RBI double, and Nunez added an RBI single.

Zach Britton replaced Sabathia to start the fourth, and Christian Vazquez greeted him with a homer to right. That would be all the runs the Red Sox would score, and all the runs they needed.

After Porcello's departure, Boston used Matt Barnes, Ryan Brasier and ace Chris Sale – who retired the Yankees in order in the eighth – to bridge to Kimbrel.

Craig Kimbrel (46) and third baseman Eduardo Nunez celebrate after the Red Sox beat the New York Yankees 4-3 in Game 4 of the ALDS, clinching a spot in the ALCS versus the Astros.

After the game, Cora first spoke of the Yankees.

"I want to congratulate the New York Yankees, Aaron Boone, Brian Cashman, and the Steinbrenner family," Cora said. "That's a great team.

"All throughout the season, it was back and forth, great games, and I think we gave the audience and the baseball world a great show. So congratulations on a great season, a great series, and the future is bright for them."

Cora then noted that the Red Sox needed everybody they had to win the series.

"Like I've been saying all along, we're a complete team, and we count on everybody to win games," Cora said. "The last two games, if you think about it, it was fun to watch." ■

Opposite: Boston Red Sox first baseman Steve Pearce stretches for the throw to the bag ahead of New York Yankees' Gleyber Torres for the final out of Game 4. Above: The Red Sox celebrate in the locker room after beating the hated Yankees 4-3 and punching their ticket to the ALCS.

The Red Sox swarm the field at Yankee Stadium after securing a spot in the ALCS for the first time since 2013.

American League Championship Series

American League Championship Series
Game 1 • October 13, 2018 • Boston, Massachusetts
Astros 7, Red Sox 2

Ice Cold

Boston's Offense Struggles Against Verlander in Cool Weather

Chris Sale vs. Justin Verlander is the kind of pitching matchup that gets the baseball world excited even if it's on a Wednesday night in June. This time when the pair of aces squared off, it took place on the Fenway Park mound in Game 1 of the American League Championship Series.

Verlander had compiled a 16-9 record with a 2.52 ERA and 290 strikeouts in his first full season with the Astros in 2018. Sale had gone 12-4 with a 2.11 ERA and 237 strikeouts for the Red Sox.

Talk about clash of the Titans.

Typical of said matchups, any number of little things can go wrong to derail either of the aces' brilliance. Game 1 turned out to be one of those games in which little went right for the Red Sox, despite the raucous of 38,007 that watched in 50-degree temperatures under clear skies.

Boston appeared as though they might strike the first blow when Mookie Betts singled to right to open the Red Sox first. One out later, he moved to second on a wild pitch before J.D. Martinez walked bringing Xander Bogaerts to the plate. But Bogaerts ended any hopes in the first when he grounded into a 6-4-3 inning-ending double play.

Boston's night digressed from there.

Sale had issued an eight-pitch walk to leadoff batter George Springer in the first, but escaped with no damage. The blade-thin southpaw wasn't as fortunate in the second.

After striking out Tyler White to start the inning and retiring Marwin Gonzalez on a line out to second, Sale walked Carlos Correa. Making matters worse, he hit the next batter Martin Maldonado before walking Josh Reddick to load the bases. Springer then stepped to the plate for his second at-bat.

"Anytime you're facing somebody like Sale, it's a grind from the first pitch on," Springer said. "So it's just kind of one of those things where you grind out an at-bat and hope for something good to happen."

It did.

Springer delivered a two-run single that he blistered past Red Sox third baseman Eduardo Nunez, on a play some thought Nunez should have made.

Clearly, Sale wasn't himself, bringing back memories of a year earlier when the Astros had been unkind to him in Game 1 of the 2017 American League Division Series. He'd surrendered seven earned runs in five innings in a Red Sox loss. In Game 4 of that same series, he pitched in relief and allowed two runs in the Red Sox's 5-4 loss that allowed the Astros to claim the series 3-1.

Sale lasted just four innings, allowing two runs on a hit and four walks while striking out five. But he did not take a loss as the Red Sox fought back to tie the game at 2 after Mitch Moreland drew a bases-loaded walk, and Jackie Bradley Jr. scored on a Verlander wild pitch.

Andrew Benintendi reacts to a strike three call in the fifth inning in Game 1 of the ALCS; it was one of Justin Verlander's six strikeouts.

Andrew Benintendi got called out looking to end the rally.

"That inning I had kind of lost my feel a bit," Verlander said. "Couldn't point a finger to why. But just to be able to execute a pitch there and get out of the inning. After the curveball before I thought it was close whether he swung or not. I thought maybe he did, maybe he didn't. I don't know. I was rooting hard for the swing, obviously."

Benintendi and Alex Cora did not agree with the strike call. The Red Sox manager took issue with home plate umpire James Hoye and was ejected accordingly.

"I was arguing balls and strikes and he threw me out," Cora said. "...I mean, I guess Verlander executed his pitch and he called it strike. Andrew didn't agree. I didn't agree. It's a big pitch right there. It's ball four, bases loaded. They got Pressly in the bullpen. Most likely Verlander comes out of the game.

"But you can't argue balls and strikes. And I did. It's kind of like embarrassing that it happens in the playoffs. That wasn't cool watching the game in the clubhouse. I got a job to do and manage the team in the dugout. But sometimes you gotta do what you gotta do and you've got to defend your players. And at least Andrew stayed in the game and he had a few more at-bats and he played left field while I was watching in my office."

Houston quickly broke the tie with a little help from Nunez.

Joe Kelly hit Alex Bregman to start the Astros' sixth. Yuli Gurriel then hit what appeared to be a scripted double-play ball to Nunez, but he bobbled the ball and all runners were safe. Two outs later, Correa singled to left to drive home Bregman and put the Astros up 3-2.

Josh Reddick led off the top of the ninth with a home run against Brandon Workman, and before the inning was over, the Astros held a 7-2 lead that would stand. ■

Jackie Bradley Jr. scores on a wild pitch during the fifth inning of Game 1 of the ALCS.

American League Championship Series
Game 2 • October 14, 2018 • Boston, Massachusetts
Red Sox 7, Astros 5

The Price is Right

Red Sox Get Gutsy Win, Even Series at 1-1

Sometimes the outcome of a game can come down to how the ball bounces. That's literally what happened in Game 2 of the American League Championship Series at Fenway Park. That, and a little help from an ace who had struggled during postseasons past.

Trailing the Astros 1-0 in the series, Boston skipper Alex Cora handed the ball to David Price to start Game 2.

Normally, having Price on the mound translated to excellence. But the former Cy Young Award winner's postseason numbers had been dismal. In 10 career postseason starts, Price had never recorded a win and neither had his teams on the nights he'd started, which translated to an 0-10 mark when he'd stepped onto the bump.

Cora wasn't buying the idea that Price put too much pressure on himself.

"I don't think that's the issue," Cora said. "I do feel that there's a few things that he got away from the last few starts. And we do feel that in Game 2 he'll get back to attack hitters in a certain way.

"That's the beauty of David. He can attack you in different ways but sometimes everything blends together, not only velocity-wise but location-wise. And Big League hitters take advantage of that. But we do feel that he'll get back to that guy that pitched from the All-Star break all the way until mid-September and he'll be fine."

The numbers backed Cora. Price had gone 6-1 with a 2.25 ERA in 11 starts after the All-Star Game. And

in Game 2, he certainly looked more like the guy who had enticed the Red Sox to sign him to a seven-year, $217-million deal prior to the 2016 season.

Along the way, Price survived innings such as the first when he issued one-out walks to Jose Altuve and Alex Bregman before recovering to strike out Yuli Gurriel looking and Tyler White swinging to end the threat.

Price again found trouble in the second. After allowing a one-out single to Carlos Correa, Martin Maldonado doubled to put runners at second and third. Josh Reddick went down on a pop out to second to bring George Springer to the plate, and he delivered a two-run double that tied the game at 2.

Marwin Gonzalez then touched Price for a two-run homer in the fourth that put the Astros up 4-2.

Boston's offense took care of matters in the bottom half of the third when Xander Bogaerts singled with one out. Steve Pearce followed with a double then Rafael Devers drew a walk to load the bases. One out later, Jackie Bradley Jr. took his second at-bat of the evening after grounding out in the first with the bases loaded. This time he doubled to left on a ball that seemed to seemed to have a mind of its own, bounding every which way. Bradley's double emptied the bases to put the Red Sox up 5-4.

"First at-bat, I think [getting the double in his second at-bat] kind of starts back with that, I saw a lot of off-speed pitches with the bases loaded," Bradley said. "Second at-bat, got started off with a fastball and saw

Often criticized for his postseason performance, David Price stepped up as the starting pitcher in the Game 2 victory.

> **That was big. Going back to the second inning when I had an opportunity to have a shut-down inning and wasn't able to do that, giving up the two-out double to Springer, that stung. But to be able to go out there in that fourth and to have a clean inning, that was good for myself and good for our team.**
>
> — *Price*

another off-speed pitch and I was in a hitter's count. So I just wanted to not do too much, see a pitch in the zone that I could handle and I got it on the 2-1 count."

As for the action the ball took? Bradley allowed that he'd never seen such a bizarre tact since he'd hit one that caromed off a Fenway Park ladder.

"I want to say that was two years ago or maybe a year ago," Bradley said. "But it's pretty cool. I've never seen it ride the top of that little edge like that before. It's pretty unique."

Taking the mound with a one-run lead, Price came through in the fourth, retiring in order Maldonado, Reddick, and Springer.

"That was big," said Price of the fourth. "Going back to the second inning when I had an opportunity to have a shut-down inning and wasn't able to do that, giving up the two-out double to Springer, that stung. But to be able to go out there in that fourth and to have a clean inning, that was good for myself and good for our team."

When Price issued a two-out walk in the fifth to White, putting runners at first and second, Cora decided

A throwing error by Astros pitcher Gerrit Cole to Yuli Gurriel allowed Xander Bogaerts to reach second base in the first inning of Game 2.

> **It wasn't the line I dreamed up to have tonight. But our offense, our defense, everybody rallied together. That's what we've done all year. Whenever starters needed to be picked up, they picked us up and vice versa. So that was big.**
>
> — *David Price*

to turn the game over to the bullpen. Price's final line: four runs on five hits, four walks, and five strikeouts in 4 2/3 innings. Price, who had been an object of the Fenway boo birds from time to time, received a standing ovation leaving the mound.

"[The ovation was] definitely appreciated," Price said. "It wasn't the line I dreamed up to have tonight. But our offense, our defense, everybody rallied together. That's what we've done all year. Whenever starters needed to be picked up, they picked us up and vice versa. So that was big."

Boston employed four relievers to cover the final 13 outs to finish off the 7-5 win that tied the series at one game each.

"We won," said Price, who did not earn the decision. "That's my first team win [in the postseason] as a starter. So if it's baby steps, it's baby steps. I expect to win. But I'm very happy that we won." ∎

Mookie Betts scores on a passed ball in the seventh inning for his second run of Game 2 of the ALCS.

American League Championship Series
Game 3 • October 16, 2018 • Houston, Texas
Red Sox 8, Astros 2

Taking Control

Bradley's Slam Powers Red Sox Over Astros in Game 3

Tied at one game each, the American League Championship Series shifted to Houston for Game 3 at Minute Maid Park.

A year earlier, Red Sox manager Joe Cora had served as Astros manager A.J. Hinch's bench coach, sitting alongside Hinch as the Astros won their first World Series in seven games over the Dodgers.

Entering the critical Game 3, Cora explained that he'd experienced any sentimentality from the past during the regular season, and he had moved on.

Houston is "a great place," Cora said. "It's a great organization. I have a lot of friends over there. But what they want is what I want. This is different, this is playoffs. And for how much, quote/unquote, they like me and they care about me, right now it's the Red Sox against the Astros.

"We will always be linked together because it was a special year last year. Not only on the field but off the field. But now it's a little bit different. We have a job to do and they do too."

Cora's job began with penciling in his starter, Nathan Eovaldi. Selecting the hard-throwing right-hander from nearby Alvin, Texas, proved to be the perfect choice.

Boston's suddenly explosive offense gave Eovaldi a two-run lead before he ever took the mound, thanks to an RBI double by J.D. Martinez and an Xander Bogaerts ground out that drove home another.

Eovaldi, who the Red Sox acquired from the Tampa Bay Rays just before the July 31 trade deadline, looked a little shaky in the first when he allowed singles to Jose Altuve and Alex Bregman in advance of a single to right by Marwin Gonzalez that scored Altuve. But Eovaldi managed to minimize the damage, retiring Josh Reddick on a fly out to end the inning.

What followed was domination from Eovaldi. Before his night was complete, he allowed two runs on six hits while striking out four in six innings, leaving with a 3-2 lead, thanks to Steve Pearce's solo home run in the top of the sixth.

Using primarily a fastball that ranged between 95 mph and 101 mph, Eovaldi threw 92 pitches, of which 60 were strikes.

"Nate was outstanding," Cora said. "Like I said, stuff-wise, he's one of the best left in October. His fastball, his cutter. He didn't throw too many breaking balls. He did to Marwin. But overall a great outing.

"He didn't get caught up in the moment either. For him, I know it was a special one. He's from the area. And I bet there's a lot of people, family members in the stands. And for him to be able to slow down the game in the second inning. The game was going very fast to us in the first. And all of a sudden in the second inning he slowed it down, and he did an outstanding job."

Despite Eovaldi's performance, Game 3 remained up for grabs as it moved into the eighth inning. That's when it became "JBJ" time.

Roberto Osuna replaced Ryan Pressly to start the

Jackie Bradley Jr. launches a 386-foot grand slam in the eighth inning of Game 3.

eighth for the Astros. Bogaerts got things started for the Red Sox with a one-out single. After Pearce grounded into a force out, Rafael Devers singled. Pinch-hitter Brock Holt then reached on a hit-by-pitch, which came as the result of an overturned replay call. That loaded the bases for Mitch Moreland. Inexplicably, Osuna hit Moreland, too, to force home Pearce and bring Jackie Bradley Jr. to the plate.

Bradley had been 1-for-17 during the regular season while hitting with the bases loaded. In Game 2 he'd come through with a three-run double when he hit with the bases loaded, and once again he would be hitting with the bases juiced.

Bradley said he was hunting for a pitch up in the zone.

"Obviously … [Osuna] hit two batters," Bradley said. "And they had been attacking me in all series long – in, down, kind of out of the strike zone – so I was trying to see a pitch up in the zone that I could handle, and I got that pitch."

Bradley did what a major-league hitter is supposed to do when he gets the pitch he's looking for. He deposited the ball over the wall in right-center field for a grand slam that put away Game 3.

Bradley's grand slam was the first postseason grand slam in major league history for a player – other than the pitcher, hitting in the ninth spot of the order.

Bradley called his hit "huge."

"We're playing a really good team in Houston," Bradley said. "Runs are at a premium. We never feel like enough runs is going to be enough. So it was very, very special for us."

Bradley has "been consistent throughout the season," Cora said. "As soon as he hit it we knew that ball was gone."

Bradley deferred most credit to Eovaldi's effort in getting the 8-2 win.

"Nate did amazing," Bradley said. "He's been like the unsung hero, coming in and just filling up the zone with strikes with all his pitches, and taking it deep into, deep into the game, allowing the bullpen to rest a little bit. He's battled since pitch one and it's been a lot of fun playing behind him." ∎

Red Sox first baseman Steve Pearce shows his ability in the field, stretching to make the out on Yuli Gurriel.

American League Championship Series
Game 4 • October 17, 2018 • Houston, Texas
Red Sox 8, Astros 6

A Wild One

Red Sox Win Memorable Game 4, on the Cusp of World Series

Talk about a game that has a little bit of everything, see Game 4 of the 2018 American League Championship Series.

Given the circumstances, this game played at Houston's Minute Maid Park felt even bigger than the fourth game of the series.

Houston's backs were against the wall. The Astros had taken a 1-0 series lead in Boston, only to watch the Red Sox take a 2-1 advantage after Games 2 and 3.

Though they had the series lead, Boston's offense wasn't about to let up and got busy in the first when Rafael Devers delivered a two-out single to left off Charlie Morton to score Mookie Betts and J.D. Martinez, giving the Red Sox a 2-0 lead.

Houston's Jose Altuve tried to answer in the bottom half of the inning with an opposite-field two-run homer off Red Sox starter Rick Porcello.

But not so fast…

Betts, playing right field, leaped at the last instant to try and snag Altuve's drive, but came down empty-handed.

"I was just kind of going back, and I got a good jump on it," Betts said. "And I was pretty positive I was going to be able to catch it. But as I jumped and went over, reached my hand up, I felt like somebody was kind of pushing my glove out of the way or something. And I got to see a little bit of the replay. I guess they were going

to catch the ball and pushed my glove out of the way."

However, umpire Joe West ruled fan interference on the play, basing his decision on his belief that Betts would have caught the ball had a fan not gotten involved.

"I didn't know it was called an out," Betts said. "That's why I got it and threw it home. I guess he got the call right."

After a Crew-Chief replay review, West's call was upheld, and the Astros came away with no runs in the first.

"I don't think I was surprised [by the call] because I knew I was going to catch it," Betts said. "So I guess you could say I was kind of surprised that he – I've never seen or been part of a play like that. So I guess, yeah, you could say I was kind of surprised he made the out call. And as I watched the video, it's like he got it right because I feel like it was going in my glove for sure."

Even though the home run call went against them, the Astros' offense continued to hit. Carlos Correa's second-inning single cut the lead in half.

Xander Bogaerts answered for the Red Sox in the top of the fourth with an RBI double, but the Astros tied the game in the bottom of the inning on a solo home run by George Springer and an RBI single by Josh Reddick.

Correa's RBI single off Joe Kelly in the fifth put the Astros up 5-4, but the Red Sox bats were working too well to call it a night at four runs. Jackie Bradley Jr. once again answered the call.

During a controversial first-inning play, Mookie Betts attempts to rob Jose Altuve's home run despite interference from the Houston fans.

After Christian Vazquez doubled with two outs in the inning, Bradley homered to right off Josh James to put the Red Sox up 6-4.

"It's amazing," Red Sox manager Alex Cora said. "[Bradley] keeps working on his craft, his swing. He understands now, he's staying through the ball, hitting the ball in the air. There's no more hitting line drives into the shift. Now he hits the ball in the air.

"He's giving himself a chance, and like I said last night, all credit goes to him. He was the one, he found it and he's staying with his process and he's done an outstanding job."

Brock Holt drew a bases-loaded walk from Lance McCullers to score a run in the seventh, and Martinez singled home Betts in the eighth to push the Boston lead to 8-5.

Cora decided to go with Craig Kimbrel at that point, bringing in the Red Sox closer to start the eighth, and the Astros pushed across a run when Altuve grounded out to shortstop with one out. Kimbrel struck out Marwin Gonzalez to end the inning, making the score 8-6 heading into the ninth.

Kimbrel had three outs under his belt, could he get the final three? If so, he would do something he never had during his career: a six-out save. That prospect began to look shaky when Kimbrel walked Josh Reddick with one out in the ninth. He then walked Correa. One out later, Tony Kemp walked to load the bases, bringing Alex Bregman to the plate with two outs.

David Price, who was scheduled to start Game 5, warmed in the bullpen for the Red Sox. Cora stuck with Kimbrel.

Bregman hit a sinking liner to left field. Fearlessly, Benintendi dove and made the catch that ended the game, giving the Red Sox an 8-6 win that took 4 hours and 33 minutes to complete.

"He's our guy," said Cora of Kimbrel. "...I know it didn't look pretty, but we got 27 outs and now we move on." ∎

Red Sox closer Craig Kimbrel glares intensely during his two-inning save in Game 4 of the ALCS.

Andrew Benintendi makes a diving catch with the bases loaded for the final out in the ninth inning to seal the victory in Game 4 of the ALCS.

American League Championship Series
Game 5 • October 18, 2018 • Houston, Texas
Red Sox 4, Astros 1

Priceless

David Price and the Red Sox Win Fourth Straight, Clinch World Series Spot

David Price on three-days rest, in a playoff game – didn't sound like a great plan. Despite the left-hander's modest success in Game 2, he still allowed four runs in 4 2/3 innings. And the Red Sox had a chance to eliminate the Astros in Game 5, on the road at Minute Maid Park.

Red Sox manager Alex Cora stood by his decision, even if Price did warm up to possibly enter Game 4 in the ninth inning. And even if the Astros were sending Justin Verlander to the mound. Price was his guy.

Staff ace Chris Sale had been slated to start for the Red Sox. But after starting Game 1, he had to be hospitalized for a stomach illness. He'd been released a day later, but he wasn't quite ready to start Game 5.

"We knew [Price] was a full-go," Cora said. "I talked to him after we found out about Chris. So he was ready. Yesterday I know he threw in the bullpen, but he really didn't get hot, I think, probably at the end. So he didn't make too many pitches."

Price entered the game at 0-9 with a 6.16 ERA in 11 previous postseason starts. Not exactly the stuff to encourage a great deal of optimism. Price never wavered, striking out two of the four batters he faced in a scoreless first inning before adding a scoreless second. By the time he took the mound to start the third, the Red Sox held a 1-0 lead thanks to J.D. Martinez.

With one out in the third, Verlander got ahead 0-2 in the count against the Red Sox slugger, and then appeared to strike him out with a third-pitch slider. Home-plate umpire Chris Guccione thought otherwise and called the pitch ball one. Martinez then homered on a curveball.

Pitching with the lead, Price took the mound in the third and retired the side in order. He added scoreless innings in the fourth and fifth. Meanwhile, Boston's offense added to the lead.

Mitch Moreland doubled to open the sixth and Ian Kinsler followed with a single to right. Verlander went with his fastball to the next batter, Rafael Devers, delivering a 98.2 mph offering. Devers swung and drove the pitch over the wall in left-center field to put the Red Sox up 4-0.

Price retired the Astros in order in the sixth, then called it a night after 93 pitches, of which 65 were strikes.

"From pitch one, I just had that feeling tonight was going to be that night for [Price]," Jackie Bradley Jr. said. "And I couldn't ask for a better teammate, the way he's battled through and the whole postseason talk, this and that. I think it really shows the determination and the competitor that's inside of him to come out here and do it against arguably the top two, three teams in baseball. We needed that performance from him tonight.

"I feel like he needed that performance for him tonight. And I don't think he's going to forget it. I know I'm not."

David Price, who struck out nine Astros while allowing just three hits in Game 5, fields Jake Marisnick's grounder in the fifth inning.

"

I definitely felt good on the mound. I continued to tell myself: Just stay in the moment. Don't worry about the next hitter. Don't think about the next pitch. Just stay right here. And I was able to do that tonight. And it paid off. And that was one of the more special nights I've ever had on the baseball field.

— David Price

"

In Price's six innings of work, he allowed no runs on three hits and no walks while striking out three to earn his first postseason win.

"I definitely felt good on the mound," Price said. "I continued to tell myself: Just stay in the moment. Don't worry about the next hitter. Don't think about the next pitch. Just stay right here. And I was able to do that tonight. And it paid off. And that was one of the more special nights I've ever had on the baseball field."

Cora noted that with Price, his performance is always contingent on command.

"From the get-go he had it," Cora said. "His velocity was up. He used his changeup a lot early in the game, a lot different than the first start. And I didn't feel for whatever people think, thought about David outside of the clubhouse. He threw the ball well in Boston [in Game 2]."

Matt Barnes took over for Price to start the seventh inning and retired the first two batters he faced. Marwin Gonzalez then touched him for a solo home run to left. When Tony Kemp then drew a walk, Cora called to Nathan Eovaldi.

Rafael Devers high-fives manager Alex Cora after hitting a three-run home run in the sixth inning.

Boston's Game 3 starter got pinch-hitter Josh Reddick to fly out to end the inning. Eovaldi then pitched a scoreless eighth before giving way to Craig Kimbrel in the ninth.

Kimbrel struck out Carlos Correa swinging before walking Yuli Gurriel.

Was this going to be another Kimbrel high-wire act? Not this time.

The Red Sox closer struck out Gonzalez then got Kemp to fly out to left for the final out of their 4-1 win.

Boston had punched its ticket for the 2018 Fall Classic, giving the Red Sox their fourth American League championships in 15 seasons, the best stretch of any team in the major leagues.

While winning the last four games of the ALCS, Red Sox hitters pushed across 27 runs.

"They did an outstanding job," Cora said. "Offensively amazing, battling since the fifth inning in Game 1, we started battling at-bats and trying to win every pitch. And if it wasn't in the zone, we were going to take it. And we grind and grind. And now we're going to the World Series." ■

Above: Red Sox manager Alex Cora holds the William Harridge Trophy while celebrating his team's ALCS triumph over the Astros. Opposite: The Red Sox celebrate after defeating the Astros to advance to their fourth World Series in the 21st century.

J.D. Martinez celebrates after hitting a third-inning home run off of Justin Verlander in Game 5 of the ALCS.